INTERPRETING MARITIME HISTORY AT MUSEUMS AND HISTORIC SITES

INTERPRETING HISTORY

About the Series
The American Association for State and Local History publishes the *Interpreting History* series in order to provide expert, in-depth guidance in interpretation for history professionals at museums and historic sites. The books are intended to help practitioners expand their interpretation to be more inclusive of the range of American history.

Books in this series help readers:
- quickly learn about the questions surrounding a specific topic,
- introduce them to the challenges of interpreting this part of history, and
- highlight best practice examples of how interpretation has been done by different organizations.

They enable institutions to place their interpretative efforts into a larger context, despite each having a specific and often localized mission. These books serve as quick references to practical considerations, further research, and historical information.

Titles in the Series

Interpreting Native American History and Culture at Museums and Historic Sites by Raney Bench
Interpreting the Prohibition Era at Museums and Historic Sites by Jason D. Lantzer

Interpreting African American History and Culture at Museums and Historic Sites by Max van Balgooy

Interpreting LGBT History at Museums and Historic Sites by Susan Ferentinos

Interpreting Slavery at Museums and Historic Sites by Kristin L. Gallas and James DeWolf Perry

Interpreting Food at Museums and Historic Sites by Michelle Moon

Interpreting Difficult History at Museums and Historic Sites by Julia Rose

Interpreting American Military History at Museums and Historic Sites by Marc K. Blackburn

Interpreting Naval History at Museums and Historic Sites by Benjamin J. Hruska

Interpreting Anniversaries and Milestones at Museums and Historic Sites by Kimberly A. Kenney

Interpreting American Jewish History at Museums and Historic Sites by Avi Y. Decter

Interpreting Agriculture at Museums and Historic Sites by Debra A. Reid

Interpreting Maritime History at Museums and Historic Sites by Joel Stone

INTERPRETING MARITIME HISTORY AT MUSEUMS AND HISTORIC SITES

EDITED BY JOEL STONE

ROWMAN & LITTLEFIELD
Lanham • Boulder • New York • London

Published by Rowman & Littlefield
A wholly owned subsidiary of The Rowman & Littlefield Publishing Group, Inc.
4501 Forbes Boulevard, Suite 200, Lanham, Maryland 20706
www.rowman.com

Unit A, Whitacre Mews, 26-34 Stannary Street, London SE11 4AB

British Library Cataloguing in Publication Information Available

Library of Congress Cataloging-in-Publication Data Is Available

ISBN 978-1-4422-7907-0 (cloth : alk. paper)
ISBN 978-1-4422-7908-7 (paper : alk. paper)
ISBN 978-1-4422-7909-4 (electronic)

∞™ The paper used in this publication meets the minimum requirements of American National Standard for Information Sciences—Permanence of Paper for Printed Library Materials, ANSI/NISO Z39.48-1992.

Printed in the United States of America

CONTENTS

LIST OF ILLUSTRATIONS   ix

PREFACE   xi

ACKNOWLEDGMENTS   xiii

PART I: INTRODUCTION

Chapter 1   Introduction to Maritime History   3

Chapter 2   The North American Maritime   13

Chapter 3   Boats and Ships of North America   21

PART II: CASE STUDIES

Chapter 4   Layers of Interpretation: The *Charles W. Morgan*'s Changing Role at Mystic Seaport   31
Erik Ingmundson

Chapter 5   Living Maritime History: The Historic *Belle of Louisville*   45
Kadie Engstrom

Chapter 6   Place, Industry, Recreation: Interpreting a Diverse Maritime Environment   57
Joel Stone

Chapter 7   Underwater Archaeological Preserves, Parks, and Trails: A Florida Perspective   71
Franklin H. Price

Chapter 8   Maritime Archaeology as "Evidence-Based Storytelling"   85
Daniel Harrison

Chapter 9   Campus Preservation and Shipwreck Research at Whitefish Point   99
             Bruce Lynn

Chapter 10   Curating and Exhibiting Recreational Boating   111
             John Summers

Chapter 11   Living Maritime History: Chanties, Ballads, and Folktales   125
             Joel Stone

Chapter 12   Difficult Maritime Topics   135
             Joel Stone

Chapter 13   The "Other" Aspects of Maritime Histories   141
             Joel Stone

BIBLIOGRAPHY   149

INDEX   157

ABOUT THE EDITOR AND CONTRIBUTORS   161

LIST OF ILLUSTRATIONS

Figure 3.1   This leaf has all the elements of a good boat   24

Figure 4.1   The *Charles W. Morgan* under tow   32

Figure 4.2   The *Charles W. Morgan* at Mystic Seaport   38

Figure 4.3   A whaleboat of the *Charles W. Morgan* conducted crew demonstrations   40

Figure 4.4   Ryan Leighton was selected "Stowaway"   42

Figure 5.1   The *Belle of Louisville* at a shoreside landing   46

Figure 5.2   The *Belle of Louisville* approaching her dock   48

Figure 5.3   The *Belle of Louisville*'s engine room   50

Figure 5.4   The *Belle of Louisville*'s pilot navigates the vessel   53

Figure 6.1   The schooner *J. T. Wing* became the *Museum of the Great Lakes*   59

Figure 6.2   Dossin Great Lakes Museum   60

Figure 6.3   The Content Map developed by Good Design Group   63

Figure 6.4   "Built by the River" exhibition, introductory section   65

Figure 6.5   Casework in the "Built by the River" exhibition   66

Figure 6.6   The Industry portion of the "Built by the River" exhibition   67

Figure 6.7   The "Built by the River" exhibition   68

Figure 7.1   Officers of the USS *Narcissus*   72

Figure 7.2   The iron-hulled lumber vessel *Georges Valentine*   76

Figure 7.3   The underwater plaque near the anchor of the British cargo ship *Copenhagen*   78

Figure 7.4   Shipwreck Poster   79

Figure 8.1   The St. Clair River "Flats"   86

Figure 8.2   British four-pound cannon barrel   87

Figure 8.3   A view of Detroit, July 25, 1794   89

Figure 8.4   The recovered cannon   91

Figure 8.5   The sidewheel steamer *Erie*   93

Figure 9.1   The pedestal-based tower at Whitefish Point   101

Figure 9.2   The reconstructed boat house at the Great Lakes Shipwreck Museum   102

Figure 9.3   The main gallery of the Great Lakes Shipwreck Museum   103

Figure 9.4   The story of the SS *Edmund Fitzgerald*   104

Figure 9.5   Dennis Hale, sole survivor of the *Daniel J. Morrell* sinking   106

Figure 9.6   A class lesson about how lighthouses communicate with ships   107

Figure 10.1   Double-paddle canoes and cruising sailing canoes   113

Figure 10.2   Department store retailers such as Sears were quick to see the potential market in recreational boating   115

Figure 10.3   In North America, kits, plans, and instructions have encouraged a do-it-yourself attitude   117

Figure 10.4   The history of recreational boating is an anatomy of desire and longing   118

Figure 10.5   The "Quest for Speed: The Story of Powerboat Racing" exhibition   121

Figure 10.6   The "Can I Canoe You Up the River?" exhibition   122

Figure 11.1   Folkways Records distributed sea songs and tavern ballads   127

Figure 11.2   Journalist Joe Grimm brought Ivan Walton's collection of Great Lakes sea songs out of the archives   128

Figure 11.3   Lee Murdock performs as a solo balladeer   131

Figure 11.4   Lee Murdock is included in conference panels and focus groups   132

Figure 11.5   Lee Murdock performs at Fayette, Michigan   133

PREFACE

I RECENTLY PICKED up a reference volume published two decades ago which introduced itself with, "Everyone interested in our maritime heritage will enjoy this book."

What an entré! Very broad and positive. I might have used the same ten words for the introduction to this text. Instead, with a glance, I discovered a thesis. If you're interested in *any* element of North American history or culture, then you *must* have an interest in our maritime heritage. Unfortunately, the number of Americans interested in the intricacies of waterborne transportation is diminishing. Those in the business of promoting maritime heritage understand that buried within that simple sentence are two issues faced every day, and they are intricately linked.

First, not enough people make that connection. The United States was a major player in transglobal migration and naval development, with important worldwide maritime influence after 1700. Despite its massive impact on every aspect of American history, maritime history does not get the attention it deserves: its importance to the movement of peoples and goods; the documentation of discovery and development; and the social, recreational, and commercial impact that "people in boats" represent. There are also significant technological advancements in America responsible for refined designs and unique marine architecture.

The second issue is that the pool of primary knowledge experts, both career mariners and dedicated marine historians, shrinks every year. The US maritime fleet, associated industries, legislation, and dedicated literature have fallen out of the consciences of the general public. Most people today are landsmen. There has been a per capita decrease in boat registration, fishing licenses, and spending on launch sites and harbors since data capture initiatives in the late 1990s.

People enjoy what they know. From a curatorial standpoint—if people do not connect to maritime history, they cannot enjoy your museum or presentation. Or can they? Can we interest them enough in boats, sailors, cargoes, resorts, shipwrecks, diving, port politics, marine design, and innovation to get their attention? It's an uphill battle, but involves preserving the stories we have, imaginatively reinventing those stories for tomorrow's audience, and continuing to search for fresh new stories and interpretation.

This book is intended to increase awareness of the opportunities to leverage maritime history within exhibitions, publications, and programs. It is also intended to expose readers to the maritime field, and to the innovative programs that are doing forward-looking interpretation.

JLS, 2016

ACKNOWLEDGMENTS

MANY THANKS to those who have taught me to love the maritime. It began with my parents. Then the friends who got me on boats—Uncle Bill, Mike, Tim, Steve, Buzz—and those in the professional marine business. Thanks to the many wonderful people, too numerous to mention, who individually and collectively have kept this heritage alive—in archives, in museums, and in their homes.

A significant nod to those who have helped me learn the history, archive, and museum businesses. As a communications student at the University of Detroit, administrative flexibility allowed me to tap the knowledge of an engineering professor to construct a two-semester historical research project. Thirty years later a graphic arts career transitioned to public history, resulting in a rewarding tenure with the Detroit Historical Society. To all who helped, guided, cajoled, pushed—many, many thanks.

Special recognition to the American Association of State and Local History, and Rowman & Littlefield for their dedication to the museum and historical interpretation profession, and to Bob Beatty and Charles Harmon for making sure that maritime interpretation—both military and commercial—is included in the association's offerings.

Those mentioned here and subsequently are responsible for the success of this volume. Failures in the text are ultimately the responsibility of the editor. Every effort was made to present the material in a clear, cohesive, and creative manner, further invigorating scholarship and preservation for America's maritime legacy.

This book is dedicated, as always, to my loving wife, Linda Mast Stone. She understands my passion for boats, even when I don't.

PART I

Introduction

CHAPTER 1

INTRODUCTION TO MARITIME HISTORY

SOME OF US are drawn to the forest. Others are drawn to the farm or the desert. Those of us drawn to the water are most fortunate. Seas, lakes, rivers, and swamps make up most of earth's surface, and man's interaction with water is one of the richest troves available for study, no matter the discipline.

We all have a stake in understanding America's maritime legacy. Nearly every person who migrated to North America, from prehistory to the 1950s, employed some form of water transportation to get here. Marine interests helped found all of our major coastal towns, which include Boston, New York, New Orleans, Seattle, as well as St. Louis, Omaha, and Duluth. Millions made their living by working on ships, or supplying shipping interests.

But this is by no means a dusty "heritage" story—this is vital and hugely relevant. Today, 95 percent of everything purchased in the United States—food, clothes, fuel, toys, phones, cars—is brought in by water. Without ships our economy would collapse, yet few people think of our national economy as a *maritime economy*.[1]

What Is Maritime History?

The term "maritime history" means different things to people. For the purpose of this volume, *maritime* is the broad umbrella covering cultures on land and afloat whose viability depends upon ships or shoreside commerce. Water irrigating a field in Nebraska is *not* maritime. Water floating a freighter carrying eighty thousand tons of Nebraska corn to Europe *is* maritime. *History* is understood to be anything before this moment that offers context through study and interpretation.

At the heart of the maritime world are boats, the tools that humans developed to challenge the waves and facilitate effective and efficient water transportation. But also in the mix are the people, ports, businesses and industries, financiers, weather, waves, naval engineering, cargoes, navigational skills, propulsion, investments, communications, regulations, recreations, ecologies, diet, clothing, religious traditions, songs, lore and literature—a panoply of cultural touchstones all circling back to man and vessel.

All of the elements listed in the previous paragraph could likely be found influencing lives in any small port town; the story can be broad in a very narrow space. Conversely, behind any American historic tale before 1900 there is usually a harbor or boat involved; broad national context can be created using very local maritime stories. Maritime history can be examined from so many perspectives that, in the attempt to interpret America's story, it is a valuable voice.

"Maritime history" as a recognized academic discipline is relatively new. Until the 1960s any scholarly investigation of the international marine was limited almost entirely to exploration, naval actions and economic analysis, and nearly always with a regional or national focus. Into the 1980s the academic community displayed an increasing "lack of awareness" to the maritime field, and by 1999 it was declared all but dead by concerned professionals. Similar declines were recognized in the museum community when it came to identifying professionals in "a diminishing pool of leadership candidates."[2]

Since then maritime history—in academia and public history—has enjoyed a resurrection; healthy in terms of dialog to the point that there have been pendulous shifts in opinion regarding interpretation. Initially, modern interpretation was regional, swinging in the late twentieth century toward a global focus, and recently to mixed and sometimes contentious approaches. Notably, the American Historical Association didn't recognize maritime history specializations until 2008.

In contrast, while historians were seeing the maritime niche eroded through the last century, maritime-related public history organizations were growing across the nation. Local communities and grassroots organizations, understanding the intrinsic value of the "last of the" ships, sailors, and properties, rallied the troops. Nonprofit organizations, museums, underwater preserves, and historic seaports were created to save ships, artifacts, ephemera, libraries, skills, and firsthand knowledge.

Why Is This History Important?

Alfred Mahan, an American admiral and historian, wrote in 1890, "The profound influence of sea commerce upon the wealth and strength of countries was clearly seen long before the true principles which governed its growth and prosperity were detected." American merchantmen, slavers, and fishing schooners generated a positive national gross domestic product before we knew to call it that.[3]

Profits justified investment during the colonial era, and became the foundation of economic success for the young United States. Fleets of coasting vessels—both sail and steam—worked the saltwater and freshwater ports across the continent. Expansionist policies in the late nineteenth century prompted the United States to redesign its navy, probably not anticipating the needs of two devastating world wars. Through the twentieth century, thriving multibillion dollar recreational marine industries served cruise ship customers, fishermen, and people just trying to make their rowboat or sloop go faster.

In the finest interpretive efforts, people are the key, and today's public history professionals are embracing diversity and inclusion. They need look no further than the maritime community, which has always been the earth's most diverse and cosmopolitan population. Seagoing vessels are where Caucasians, Asians, and Africans worked together for centuries melding ethnic and cultural traditions, where lords interacted with peasants as a matter of conquest, enrichment, and survival, and where the products of one continent were carefully curated for enthusiastic consumers half a world away. In one form or another, these scenarios remain intact and important.

There is a sense of urgency to capture previous eras and cultures, and a sense of the people, vessels, and their trade. Unfortunately, for some it is too late. In 1984, Neil Hollander and Harald Mertes set out to capture the final days of working sail in their book, *The Last Sailors*. They contacted harbormasters around the world, looking for active commercial sailing vessels. The response too often was, "Sorry, you're five years too late." Or, "The last one is now in a museum."[4] Most of the great shantymen have passed, as have men who understand how to operate a quadruple expansion steam engine, hand reef a topsail in a gale, or launch a harpoon from the tenuous perch in the bow of a whaleboat. Unfortunate, but perhaps the lesson to be learned is that the superships of today—seemingly gargantuan, passionless machines—are a maritime culture that should be embraced, recorded, studied, and preserved now while it is strong.

Part of the job of telling this story includes correcting long-standing misconceptions and serving as advocates for truth in interpretation. Howard Chappelle, longtime marine curator at the Smithsonian, addresses this in his *History of American Sailing Ships* in 1935. "To quote but two examples, the *Constitution* and *Flying Cloud* have been made to appear the most important and best ships of their periods, and their designers made to be supermen. This is quite unwarranted, and the false picture should be corrected. In addition, the passage of time has developed many ideas and claims . . . that have no historical foundation."[5]

He cautions that those studying today's maritime world should avoid the misconception that earlier mariners, cartographers, armorers, and shipwrights were primitive. "In order to thoroughly understand history it is necessary to realize the fact that men of earlier years had the same abilities and powers of reason and intellect that can be found in similar stations of life today." And considering the work they did without the aid of computer modeling and CAD/CAM technologies, perhaps they were even smarter than we are.

How Do Historians Approach Interpretation?

After almost a century, there are a number of interpretive theories developed to address fluid customer expectations and learning theory.

The early approach to marine history was theoretical, capturing regional politics and the involvement of navies. Regionalism remained the norm in North America as historians studying battles and commerce grappled with local histories, often capturing them as they disappeared—proving a real boon today.

Regionalism shifted to internationalism in the late twentieth century, and still has many champions. In 2009, Gelina Harlaftis described "littoral societies," shoreside units found around the world, and worthy of being compared in that model. Frank Broeze wrote that maritime history is "necessarily international in nature," and there has been strong advocacy in this regard from the *International Journal of Maritime History.* This was a healthy shift in dialog, and reflected the globalization trend popular at the close of the millennium.[6]

Extending the discussion further, Joshua Smith notes that our maritime dialog, while still international, "betrays the blue-water bias of most maritime history, a bias so strong that it is almost a defining feature."[7] Blue Water generally excludes the Mediterranean, Caribbean, gulfs, coastal and interisland trade, rivers, deltas, swamps, and the Great Lakes.

Within the last few decades proponents have separated into groups, described by Smith as traditionalists and utilitarians. Traditionalists reestablished the discipline within the scholar community—an uphill battle—and vigorously defend its respectability. Utilitarians look to maritime history to involve a broader audience, and leverage knowledge and experiential-based learning to affect training, interpretation, and policy.

These discussions took place during a self-described period of declining scholarship, but also during a period of steadily increasing community support for maritime projects. Connecticut's Mystic Seaport—originally the Marine Historical Association—was founded in 1929. The Mariners' Museum in Newport News, Virginia, opened in 1930. In tiny Fairport, Ohio, 1945 saw the ribbon cutting for the Fairport Harbor Marine Museum, the first of many Great Lakes lighthouse and maritime museums, joined by a number of regional museums opened across the country after World War II: the Museum of the Great Lakes debuted in 1949 in Detroit; Philadelphia's Independence Seaport opened in 1961; South Street Seaport in New York opened in 1967; the *Bluenose II, Pride of Baltimore, Alvin Clark,* and *Clearwater* programs launched about this time, all enjoying successes and suffering disappointments. Since then Fisherman's Wharf in San Francisco, Pier Wisconsin in Milwaukee, *Belle of Louisville* in Kentucky, and a number of other waterfront repurposing projects have extended the reach of maritime history.

These are all what Sherene Suchy describes as the "entrepreneurial museum." No longer supported entirely, or partially, by municipal tax dollars in an uncompetitive entertainment market, museum directors, trustees, and staff are creating new business models to remain relevant. After years of independence, these professionals must refocus their scholarship, positioning their organization "for long-term survival, which includes presenting the museum's story in a way that advocates its worth as a social institution," and represents integrity as well as creativity.[8]

What's the Problem?

In the minds of the early marine writers, the topics of interest seemed to be: explorers, admirals, and specific economic interests like whaling and shipbuilding, pirates, heroism, and disasters. Today that remains the norm. Maritime for public consumption is *Master and Commander,* Captain Hook, *Amistad, Moby Dick* (or recently the *Essex* saga), Jack Sparrow, *Finest Hours, Titanic,* or the latest shipwreck video on YouTube. So really, not much has changed.

Except that, despite the explosive growth of museums in recent years, the number of places offering maritime scholarship and interpretation has fallen—in the museum world below 3 percent. So the question might be: If the nation's general understanding of ships and the sea has held a consistent and sensational place in our culture, why has interest in solid maritime history waned? Why has the historical community been unable to broaden the understanding of the ships, the ocean, and the effect they have on our lives?

It might be as simple as this: When the majority of Americans lived within walking distance of a wharf, and when the fantastic sailing frigates and clipper ships represented the height of American technology and economic reach, everyone had a connection with the sea that was tangible and real. Your great uncle sailed with Farragut or Dewey; An immigrant survived the tough North Atlantic on a tramp steamer. A platoon jumped from a landing ship at Omaha Beach; A town set its clocks by the punctual steam whistle of the departing riverboat. Newsreels covered a famous movie star's arrival in New York by ocean liner. Ships were part of the everyday equation.

Today, by comparison, if you have an aunt or uncle in the navy, they will appear more professional than nautical. When there is a commodity shortage, seldom does a ship come to mind as the cause. Immigrants, soldiers, and movie stars arrive or depart on jets, and everyone's clock is their phone. Ships are no longer part of America's daily experience.

There is a psychological barrier; a lack of involvement and connection between Americans and the sea. Because of this disconnect, the historical community must vigilantly pursue fresh interpretation, careful preservation, and an increased profile. Many of our colleagues are doing imaginative things to draw more visitors closer to their nautical family. New technologies are being creatively employed to add fresh layers to our understanding of the past, and offer this knowledge to ever broader audiences, while simultaneously increasing protections for maritime heritage assets.

Maritime research has been multidisciplinary for decades. Increasingly, archaeologists, anthropologists, historians, archivists, librarians, educators, and divers cooperate toward a common goal. Dan Harrison's chapter on evidence-based interpretation is an enlightening story of opportunity being recognized and realized by leveraging a myriad of tools available across various professional disciplines. In all the chapters, partnerships—both public and private—are keys to success.

Good work is being done across the country; however, this historical niche is hugely undervalued in the nation's cultural budget. As of 2014, there were over thirty-five thousand museums, zoos, and cultural attractions in the United States, according to the Institute for Museum and Library Services.[9] Slightly over half—about nineteen thousand—of those facilities focused on history or historic preservation.[10] The 2007 listing from Robert Smith's *Maritime Museums of North America* identifies about 650 US institutions that actively promote maritime history. That number is up from 610 a decade earlier, an encouraging trend that includes sites in forty-three states.[11] However, it represents less than 3 percent of historical interpretation nationally.

Smith's list includes museums, large and small, but also lighthouses, museum ships, libraries and archives, and physical features like canal parks and locks. Few of these institutions receive significant government funding; most are operated by local nonprofit organizations relying on grants, donations, facility rentals, and tours. The Council of American Maritime Museums (CAMM), representing the top-tier interpretive entities, has a membership of seventy-two in 2016.[12]

While these figures are disturbingly low, there are signs that the shift over the last fifty years has had positive elements, if only modest ones. The profession in America has expanded the diversity of its interpretation, but historian Lincoln Paine notes the over-whelming Anglo-oriented approach to maritime literature.[13] Only in the last decade or so have other voices been brought into the choir. While maritime history has little profile at America's top fifty universities, Joshua Smith notes that America has more maritime historians than any other country. Those two facts suggest that the nautical conversation at the higher levels of scholarship has not maintained its spark, but there is interest within both the scholarly and public history worlds that is not getting sufficient attention.

What Can Be Learned from Museum Interpretation Theory?

The fact that American maritime museums are a tiny fraction of the total indicates that, compared to the rest of the history world, not much research or attention has been paid to this niche's interpretation. Historians, at least within the United States, currently favor regionalism within a national and international context. Most museum folk would agree with that approach: grab people where they live, get them interested in what they know, then offer layers of new information, expanding their worldview.

This discussion is old, but never tired.[14] Over the last two decades the conversation has blossomed. Research, books, papers, and proponents espouse endless approaches to your audience, but they invariably insist you must *approach* your audience. Old museums were designed around content; put it up and let them appreciate it. New museums are designed around the visitor; how they appreciate history dictates the best ways to attract them to content.

So how does your visitor appreciate history? John Falk and Lynn Dierking suggested a museum-based model in the early 1990s that is applicable in several disciplines. It assesses three components of the visitor: the personal context, the social context, and the physical context. Personal refers not only to affinity and knowledge, but expectations and agenda. Public museum visits are always social, and the overall experience varies based on who you are sharing the space with. Physical elements can be environmental—size, shape, light, sound, navigation—or simply the selection of that environment to complement another agenda. Together, these three components—personal, social, and physical—in various proportions, create the visitor experience.[15]

Today the discussion is much livelier. Is a department store a better museum than a museum? Centrally and strategically located, it has something for everyone, items on demand, free admission, and is highly attuned to customer needs.[16] Can a museum be self-curated *ad infinitum*? Or entirely mobile or electronic? Or entirely underwater? Does it thrive on its physical presence? Or thrive on reinterpreting physical presence? And the biggest questions: What will our visitors expect to see in twenty years, and how can the industry help shape those expectations?

Should they expect to be educated? Funders certainly expect that, but most visitors don't cite that as their primary reason for visiting. The late entertainer Johnny Carson is said to have noted that people will pay more to be entertained than educated. By extension, they want to enjoy the social and participatory aspects of their visit. Some *expect* the community, in some manner, to support this entertainment, even as government- and foundation-based expenditures on museums (and education in general) are in steady decline, mirroring museum attendance.

Theoretically, the public history profession still holds education at its core. In 2014, Elizabeth Merritt, founding director of the American Alliance of Museum's Center for the Future of Museums, flatly stated, "Museums are educational powerhouses," spending more than $2 billion annually on educational initiatives. Barry Lord, editor of 2007's *The Manual of Museum Learning*, declared that "Museum learning is a vital component of the lifelong learning that we now perceive as essential to the development of both the individual and his or her society." Even so, curators, educators, and docents understand that, to reach that goal, their exhibitions, programs, and tours must engage the audience in participatory and provocative ways—they want to be entertained. The positive result of this, according to Nina Simon in *The Participatory Museum*, is that the more accustomed guests become to being provoked and participating, the more they want to be involved. Faced with declining attendance, this approach seems to logically address community education concerns and museum relevance.[17]

All of these factors are pertinent to interpretation of the "limited" world of the North American maritime. This volume is meant to elevate this topic in our cultural institutions, and make it as important as the historical record—past and present—suggests it should be. The chapters that follow expand the discussions regarding education, mobility, technology, diversity, physical material and spaces, broad expectations and needs—and even free admission and self-curation.

What Can Be Learned from Current Maritime Interpretation?

Chapters 4 and 5 in this volume address the active and evolving approaches for presenting historic vessels to the public. Ships are the most easily grasped "maritime" objects in the public mind, and a great starting point. Erik Ingmundson's introductory chapter describes the transformative journey—figuratively and literally—of the whaling ship *Charles W. Morgan* from a scrapyard prospect, to the iconic centerpiece of a living history site, to an engaging and mobile maritime ambassador. Over the last seventy-five years, the *Morgan* has been the subject of ongoing preservation and conservation initiatives related to Connecticut's Mystic Seaport, the pillar of experiential learning opportunities, and recently the focus of an intense and imaginative pan-organizational experiment in cross-disciplinary marketing and education.

By comparison, Kadie Engstrom, education coordinator aboard the equally iconic *Belle of Louisville*, examines a commercial enterprise based aboard the oldest operating Mississippi River–style steamboat in the world. Like the *Morgan*, the *Belle* is the last of her kind in America and recognized as a National Historic Landmark. Unlike the

Morgan, the *Belle* is not supported by a living history site, an elite historical collection, an extensive public history staff, or a dense population corridor. The *Belle* is a working vessel manned by professional mariners, and must earn her keep doing what she has done for over a century—navigating the currents and hazards of a living river system through a demanding spring-to-autumn season in America's heartland.

The sixth chapter examines one museum's effort to tell a broad maritime story in a limited space. During a 2013 renovation of the Dossin Great Lakes Museum in Detroit, the Detroit Historical Society team addressed the city's centuries-long maritime heritage in a single room: from prehistoric fishing villages to *BassMaster* magazine tournaments, fur trade canoes to Gold Cup hydroplanes, shipyards and foundries to resort hotels, and US Navy to the Canadian Coast Guard. Using "Place," "Commerce," and "Recreation" as overall themes, various interpretive tools were employed to draw most—not all, by any means—elements into the gallery. By all accounts the installation has been a success, and that success is the result of a defined interpretive process. This chapter is a brief discussion of that process.

Two more of the chapters explore our nation's underwater assets as sources of, and places for, innovative interpretation. And you don't have to be a diver to enjoy the benefits. Franklin Price's examination of Florida's underwater preserves system is the story of community partnerships and effective technologies coming together to elevate underwater wreck sites on the public's entertainment radar. The Florida project is one of two in the country—the other in Michigan—that successfully promotes significant bottomland protections for historic research and recreation. Cooperation between municipal Florida governments and dive shops in close proximity to wreck sites, as well as state and federal agencies promoting tourism and preservation, create enough interest and funding to maintain the program. Perhaps more important, Florida's system makes its assets easily available to the nondiving public worldwide through online resources.

Daniel Harrison's piece, alluded to earlier, beautifully illustrates how subsurface material culture, cutting edge technologies, and historical records can be used to develop "evidence based storytelling." By finding, examining, and analyzing the time capsules on North America's bottomlands, often untouched for centuries even in highly developed urban areas, new and exciting insights can be drawn to guide maritime interpretation—insights that are otherwise not available to terrestrial researchers. These maritime stories have relevance to a wide variety of social and cultural discussions, enhancing interpretation across a broad spectrum.

Bruce Lynn's reflection on Whitefish Point also includes shipwrecks, but more closely ties with this writer's observations about challenges posed when telling multiple stories in a single space. In Lynn's case, the "space" is a remote government lighthouse facility along Lake Superior's eastern Shipwreck Coast. The Great Lakes Shipwreck Historical Society is dedicated to disseminating information on the many wreck sites in their area. Since 1978 they have documented numerous structures and artifacts, restored an active lighthouse, retired life-saving station and fog building, and created an interpretive-center-in-the-wilderness that addresses their primary mission. Hundreds of thousands of people trek to this unique interpretive "space" each year, during a short summer season. Many are repeat visitors, which is probably not a coincidence.

Recreational boating is an element of maritime history often missed or treated as fluff. Certainly, this segment represents fun and relaxation, but it is also a significant economic generator. Most of the boats bought in North America have been built on the continent, and fishing tournaments, sailing regattas, and canoe races all drive significant tourist dollars. Historically, waterborne recreation is hugely diverse in nature, and John Summers brings extensive career experience to his discussion of the myriad ways to approach the topic.

There is a chapter on employing music to interpret the American maritime, written after a lifetime of experience and a delightful conversation with purveyors Lee Murdock and Joann Murdock. While other industries generated a rich contribution to music literature—coal mining and railroads come to mind in North America—only sailors actively engaged in singing to carry on their work and record the vagaries and minutia of their lives. Sea songs and associated shoreside tavern fare offer a primary resource for eighteenth- and nineteenth-century culture that is colorful, insightful, focused, sadly terminal, but largely untapped outside of maritime history circles. Lee and Joann have been promoting this music for decades. Lee lends advice from the research and performance side; Joann from the business opportunity side.

Top-of-mind for historical interpreters recently have been approaches to difficult history, avoided for many years and now embraced, enthusiastically if cautiously. A short chapter looks at a number of maritime topics that can be difficult to address for a variety of reasons.

The final chapter validates many other aspects included in the epithet "maritime history." The physical constraints of this volume prompted an editorial decision to deliver depth to eight specific interpretive challenges, through the case studies in chapters five through twelve. However, the breadth of the topic demands at least a review of related processes, places, and thoughts that could benefit this discussion. These include: military history and maritime remembrance; Native American maritime cultures; the role of maritime in the Underground Railroad; various North American ethnic immigrant groups and their relationship with the water; and elements of history that are seldom linked to boats or ships in public perception.

Notes

1. Rose George, *Ninety Percent of Everything: Inside Shipping, the Invisible Industry* (New York: Metropolitan Books, 2013); The Maritime Administration and the U.S. Marine Transportation System, "A Vision for the 21st Century" accessed February 2016, http://www.marad .dot.gov/wp-content/uploads/pdf/Vision_of_the_21st_Century_10-29.pdf.

2. Daniel Vickers, "Beyond Jack Tar," *William and Mary Quarterly* (3rd Series) 50:2 (April 1993): 418; Joshua M. Smith, "Far Beyond Jack Tar: Maritime Historians and the Problem of Audience," *Coriolis* 2(2) (2011): 1, accessed February 2016, http://ijms.nmdl.org/article/ view/9836; Sherene Suchy, *Leading with Passion: Change Management in the 21st Century Museum* (Walnut Creek, CA: AltaMira, 2004), 8.

3. Alfred Thayer Mahan, *The Influence of Sea Power on History, 1660–1783* (London: Little, Brown, 1890).

4. Neil Hollander and Harald Mertes, *The Last Sailors: The Final Days of Working Sail* (New York: St. Martin's, 1984), xi.

5. Howard I. Chappelle, *History of American Sailing Ships* (New York: W.W. Norton, 1935), 2–3.

6. Gelina Harlaftis, "Maritime History or the History of *Thalassa*," in *The New Ways of History*, ed. Gelina Harlaftis, Nikos Karapidakis, Kostas Sbonias, and Vaios Vaiopoulus (IB Tauris, London 2009), 211–38; Frank Broeze, *Maritime History at the Crossroads: A Critical Review of Recent Historiography* (St. John's, Newfoundland: International Maritime Economic History Association, 1995), xix.

7. Smith, "Beyond Jack Tar," 2.

8. Suchy, *Leading with Passion*, 18–20.

9. Institute of Museum and Library Services (IMLS), "Government Double Official Estimate; There Are 35,000 Active Museums in the U.S.," accessed February 2016, https://www.imls.gov/news-events/news-releases/government-doubles-official-estimate-there-are-35000-active-museums-us.

10. IMLS, "Distribution of Museums by Discipline," accessed February 2016, https://www.imls.gov/assets/1/AssetManager/MUDF_TypeDist_2014q3.pdf.

11. Robert H. Smith. *Maritime Museums of North America and Canada* (New York: Finley-Greene Publications, 1998), xv–xxxv; Smith, *Maritime*, 2007 updates accessed February 2016, http://www.maritimemuseums.net/.

12. Council of American Maritime Museum Membership List, accessed February 2016, https://councilofamericanmaritimemuseums.org/member-directory/.

13. Lincoln Paine, "Beyond Dead Whales: Literature of the Sea and Maritime History," *IJMH* 22, no. 1 (June 2010): 205–8.

14. Kathleen McLean, "Do Museum Exhibitions Have a Future?" in *Reinventing the Museum*, ed. Gail Anderson (Lanham, MD: AltaMira, 2012), 291–301.

15. John H. Falk and Lynn D. Dierking, *The Museum Experience* (Washington, D.C.: Whalesback Books, 1992).

16. John Cotton Dana, "The Gloom of the Museum," in *Reinventing the Museum*, ed. Gail Anderson (Lanham, MD: AltaMira, 2012), 17–33.

17. Elizabeth Merritt, "Setting the Stage," in *Building the Future of Education*, accessed September 2016, http://www.aam-us.org/docs/default-source/center-for-the-future-of-museums/building-the-future-of-education-museums-and-the-learning-ecosystem.pdf?sfvrsn=2, 9; Barry Lord, *The Manual of Museum Learning* (Lanham, MD: AltaMira, 2015), 3; Nina Simon, *The Participatory Museum* (Santa Cruz, CA: Museum 2.0, 2010), ii.

CHAPTER 2

THE NORTH AMERICAN MARITIME

IT HAS LONG been speculated that the first humans to arrive in North America walked from Asia via the Bering Land Bridge fifteen thousand years ago. More recent scholarship argues the likelihood that the first, and subsequent, migrants arrived by boat about the same time, with evidence—physical, genetic, cultural, lingual—suggesting that the *entrepont* were the Pacific Ocean coast of South America and North America's Atlantic Ocean. What is pretty certain is that over several millennia—until the 1960s—almost everyone who came arrived by boat.

North America's earliest mariners, like primitive mariners everywhere, started small. Their traditions were regional and dictated by available materials, functional needs, and navigational conditions. Skin-over-frame boats were popular to the north, where wood was scarce and hide plentiful. Across the continent's mid-section, bark-over-frame construction created sturdy and economical vessels which reached far into rivers and streams, harvesting rice and furs. To the south, where wood was abundant but rotting wood was a constant problem, short-lived bark boats, dugout canoes, and rafts were all viable.

European sailors arriving prior to the eighteenth century depended on their own maritime traditions for transatlantic travel, bringing with them the tools, materials, and hardware necessary to maintain their ships. Nordic adventurers explored the continent's northern coast, followed by Mediterranean-based incursions to the south, and European empirical ventures midcontinent.

Among the important physical records of early Europeans in North America are those of the Mediterranean's trading routes. Atlantic coast ports enriched Spanish and Portuguese markets with exports of gold, silver, and agricultural products. There is evidence of Indonesian explorers engaging South Americans on the Pacific side, but no similar interaction to the north.

As the Spanish maritime waned, French, Dutch, and British, then American, interests came to dominate the coastal trade. French interests populated the northern St.

Lawrence River and Atlantic ports, as well as the Mississippi Gulf. Gradually, Dutch and English settlements thrived from Massachusetts to the Carolinas. Frenchmen on the continental interior adapted Native bark canoes for commerce, and they remained efficient transportation options until the early twentieth century. Other Europeans melded their traditional shipbuilding methods with the demands of local navigation, building shallower craft with more efficient sail designs for coasting and fast deep-draught boats for the transatlantic trade.

The ocean boats became the basis for five important industries based out of the American maritime colonies. Initially there was the simple, but important, cross-Atlantic package trade, carrying what historian T. H. Breen referred to as the "baubles of Britain," satisfying North American tastes—French, Dutch, English, and later German and Irish—with those items considered luxurious or familiar, many brought in by smugglers. Deep-hulled vessels also carried molasses, rum, and slaves in the notorious Triangle Trade to the Caribbean Islands; maintained the world's most robust whale fishery; and caught codfish with such profitable efficiency that the species was nearly eliminated. Prior to the American Civil War, American ship design rivaled the finest yards in the British Empire, turning out highly refined vessels, termed Clipper Ships, that could dash to China and back with the fresh teas and spices vital to European food tastes. These new maritime routes upset an ancient terrestrial trade along the trans-Asian Silk Road, and along with the other new maritime markets shifted the balance of world financial power.

Britain dominated the world's waterways during the late eighteenth century, but was challenged around the globe by American merchant fleets during the entire nineteenth century. With the beginning of the twentieth century, American warships challenged British and German hegemony.

The US Navy had been born of necessity prior to the War of 1812, and proved itself worthy during that conflict. Prior to the Civil War the institution grew slowly, but established professionalism in its training with the birth of the Naval Academy at Annapolis, and revisions to antiquated methods of promotion and seniority. The fleet began the important transition from sail to steam, paddlewheels to propellers, and wood construction to iron. Naval assets were used to advance scientific and political concerns, including creation of the naval observatory and hydrographic office, expansion of the lighthouse service, exploration of undiscovered parts of the earth particularly to the north and south, and nation building forays highlighted by Admiral Perry's exchanges with Japan starting in 1852.

Between 1854 and 1859 at least thirty new vessels were added to the existing eighteen, six being state-of-the-art steam frigates. With the coming of war in 1861, the navy had ninety ships on its list, but only forty-two were in commission, and at least twenty-one were unserviceable.[1] It enjoyed a standing pool of officers, and had little trouble drawing deckhands from commercial shipping into the service. By comparison, the Confederate States Navy, built from scratch, suffered from a lack of ships and seamen. The South had only three shipyards—the main naval yard at Newport, Virginia, captured from the Union early on, was significant—and only one sizable foundry. However, there was very little in the way of maritime industry, and therefore no skilled labor force. They received limited support from Britain, mostly in the form of blockade runners financed and built to get southern cotton to British mills. While remaining officially neutral, British shipyards turned out a limited number of warships that allowed the Confederates to harass the Union and put up a spirited defense. Confederate shipyards were innovative in the face of tremendous odds, producing ironclads and gunboats despite severe material restrictions.[2]

Not surprisingly, merchant shipping during this period suffered tremendously. Confederate raiders managed to capture or destroy 237 northern ships, and many owners reflagged their vessels in neutral countries. Prior to hostilities, American ships carried 70 percent of foreign trade in the United States. By the turn of the century, that fell to just 8 percent.[3] Before moving to that chapter of American maritime development, a word must be said about growth and innovation on the Great Lakes and western rivers, as each sector experienced unique histories.

In the interior, characteristics of the waterways, resources, and the nature of the merchandise defined the vessels needed. Saltwater craft operated under the same restraints, but conditions midcontinent required a greater variety of constructions. Perhaps the most humble, the bark canoe, became the basis for one of the richest trades on the continent—fur. This was followed by a number of specialty designs—sternwheelers, paddlewheelers, propellers, bulk carriers, passenger packets—accommodating grain, lumber, cotton, tobacco, indigo, iron and copper ore, south along the Mississippi watershed and east through the Great Lakes. The antebellum fleet in each region represented hundreds of steamboats annually, and the lakes carried thousands of schooners. Some of America's finest and most efficient open-water steamers and shallow-water commercial vessels were developed independent of the saltwater maritime.

Of course, the Mississippi River and her many tributaries have two things in common: there is always a current, and water levels can vary significantly based on the season. The nature of a river system dictates that one way is down stream and the other is up. Down is easy, and this created a natural funnel for produce and manufacturing of the early west to a ready market in any town south, all the way to New Orleans. In the development of the nascent United States, the importance of this marine avenue cannot be discounted. By 1848, goods transported on the system surpassed the value of trade carried in saltwater craft.[4]

Similarly, Great Lakes commerce was expected to match that within a few years, but in a very different environment. The broad expanse of five freshwater seas spans three climate zones, extends nearly to the middle of the continent, and connects by rivers to a nearly three-hundred-thousand-mile watershed. Rivers connecting the lakes had currents, but water and ships in the basin were more susceptible to winds than currents and tides. In close proximity to the Mississippi, the two created a vast economic network extending west to the Rocky Mountains. While referred to as Lakes, they have a breadth and ferocity that have wrecked thousands of vessels and doomed tens of thousands of sailors and passengers.

In opening the American interior, explorers, farmers, miners, and entrepreneurs relied on watercraft. There were some coach routes available, done in stages—an uncomfortable way to travel in the best conditions. However, railroads did not spread their web significantly until well after the Civil War. For all immigrant communities, ships were a lifeline, bringing commodities in and taking harvests—furs, cotton, lumber, ores and aggregates—to markets around the world.

During the last third of the nineteenth century, three notable changes took place in the maritime world: iron and steel replaced wood for most ship construction; standards for boats and professional mariners increased; and a higher standard of living in the general population allowed for leisure time, fostering recreational boating. The use of iron and steel was the greatest technological change in the shipping world. Engines, communications, and navigation tools improved, but metallurgical advances created larger, sturdier, and safer vessels.

Increased professionalism was reflected in several ways. Aids to navigation—lighthouses, charts, uniform lighting and whistle signals, dredging, locks—made it easier for mariners to do their jobs. Governmental regulations, insurance inspections, and professional organizations for master, mates, and engineers addressed ship safety, training, and certification. Labor unions for deckhands and longshoremen lobbied for seniority rules, improved working conditions, and better pay. Recreationally, rowing, swimming, fishing, and sailing emerged as sports that brought people in contact with the water as never before, and the resort trade—often served by passenger steamers—entertained the middle and upper classes in style.

The American merchant fleet entered the twentieth century in a mixed situation. While less than 10 percent of US saltwater trade was carried in American "bottoms" (a professional nickname for a ship's hull), the Great Lakes trade was healthy; the Detroit River was the busiest waterway in the world, even as shipyards struggled. Western riverboat trade peaked decades earlier, but was still modestly viable. Then the Great War began.

Between 1914 and 1919, the American merchant marine ballooned. German U-boats were claiming one-in-four British cargo vessels, and US shipyards, under the Navy's Emergency Fleet Corporation, scrambled to fill the gap and keep supplies flowing to the Allies. The American Bureau of Shipping, which classified new builds for safety, dealing with about two-thirds of the US output, saw production jump from 230,000 tons in 1916 to well over three million tons in 1919. Additionally, in counterpoint to the Civil War situation, hundreds of foreign ships switched ownership to the United States, allowing some protection and access to US shipyards for maintenance and repair.

When the war ended, this glut of quickly built new construction and surplus hulls resulted in a collapse of freight prices. Many of these boats were placed in "ordinary"— laid up, sitting idle. Legislators in Washington, D.C., attempted to protect American shipping interests by passing the Merchant Marine Act of 1920, usually referred to as the Jones Act for its author, Senator Wesley Jones. This measure was intended to ensure that cargos between US ports were carried by US ships that had US owners and US crews. It was initially effective, but coastal shipping was suffering from other issues unrelated to the excess of vessels.

The early twentieth century saw the explosion of interest in automobiles. Hundreds of companies around the country produced vehicles, and Americans were fascinated. Automobile commuting, camping, and Sunday drives replaced steamboat travel. Trucks absorbed much of the regional freight traffic—that which railroads didn't control. The coastal trade that the Jones Act was meant to protect was cycling down even before the Great Depression began.

For both passengers and freight crossing the Atlantic, steamships were the only option until a few years before World War II, when transatlantic commercial air travel began. However, high profile disasters like the *Titanic* in 1912, the *Empress of Ireland* in 1914, and the *Lusitania* and *Eastland* in 1915—over 4,500 lives lost on four ships—made potential customers nervous. A great majority of commercial passenger lines on all coasts were consolidated or went out of business (or both) by 1930.

There were positive developments during this period. Radio telegraphs, ship-to-shore radios, and gyrocompasses were installed on passenger packets, and gradually on cargo vessels. Weather and condition reports improved safety, and put passengers and insurers at ease. After the *Titanic* incident, additional lifeboats, life jackets, and safety drills became mandatory. In the engine room, direct-drive, coal-fired steam was no longer the only option. Oil-fueled boilers gained popularity, and diesel or diesel-electric engines were proving efficient. Hull construction was shifting from riveting to welding, lowering production costs. Labor union successes and the La Follette Seaman's Act of 1915 improved working conditions for sailors, albeit at the expense of the ailing shipping companies. For sportsmen, gasoline engines replaced steam and naphtha in small yachts, and the speedboat was born.

Despite these bright spots, the 1920s were tough on American maritime businesses, except in the recreational sphere. The 1930s were devastating. With a glut of rotting ships, yards stood idle, barely kept open by federal subsidies. Shipbuilding was labor intensive, and people needed jobs. President Franklin Roosevelt wanted to increase the subsidies. Congress called for a cut in subsidies. A compromise was the Merchant Marine Act of 1936, which addressed defensive concerns in light of growing uncertainties in Asia and Europe. Shipyard production accelerated, although the United States was far behind Europe and Japan as World War II began.

In 1940, the US Maritime Commission had two hundred ships on order in nineteen shipyards, almost double the yards in service four years prior. In addition the British Merchant Shipbuilding Mission ordered sixty vessels to help offset the 150 lost to German torpedoes by September of that year alone; British yards were full, and Americans were building new ones. By the end of the war, an additional eighteen yards would come on line with a single purpose—to produce the 2,710 workhorse Liberty ships, totaling nearly 19.5 million gross tons.

Of course, navy yards worked overtime building and repairing, and every small boat manufacturer across the country was involved building landing craft, rescue boats, target barges, and utility boats. Marine and automotive engine manufacturers turned out power plants for PT boats (Packard) and harbor tugs (Chrysler). Ford and General Motors produced amphibious vehicles; Ford, a jeep-like boat, and GMC the famous DUKW (Ducks) in collaboration with Sparkman and Stevens yacht designers.

Arguably the tens of thousands of amphibious assault crafts (landing crafts) produced by Higgins Boat of Louisiana and Chris-Craft in three plants in Michigan—no longer than thirty-seven feet—were essential in winning both the Atlantic and Pacific wars. The history of World War II from the maritime perspective is fascinating and complex. In retrospect, what happened after the war was surprising.

American Bureau of Shipping President J. Lewis Luckenbach led the introductory remarks at the October 1944 American Merchant Marine Conference by stating that "in building this merchant marine we have proven to the world what America is and what America can do—give America opportunity and we will have no fear for the future of our American merchant marine."[5]

Initially he was correct. The need for postwar transportation was immediate, and—having learned a lesson in the First World War—the US government quickly began to divest itself of about half the fleet to countries around the world whose ships had been destroyed during the conflict. Allies got favorable financing terms and the shipping world settled toward normalcy. Luckenbach advocated for American-flagged ships to dominate the global landscape, but despite worldwide demand generated by the Marshall Plan, the growing Cold War with Russia, and conflicts in Asia, American investors didn't rally to maintain the fleet. Shipbuilding technologies fostered in North America during the war, particularly Henry Kaiser's efficiency innovations, were eschewed by American yards even as they were embraced by former allies and enemies. Both American industries—shipping and shipbuilding—went into rapid decline.

There were achievements during this period, several directly related to war technologies. Radar, radio telephony, and radio direction technologies were widely adopted and improved navigational safety. The United Nation's International Marine Organization (IMO) was formed in 1959 to govern and regulate the postwar maritime. In 1960 and 1974, the United Nations strengthened an international convention, first passed in 1914, known as *Safety of Life at Sea* (SOLAS); construction, security, and environmental guidelines and regulations that have been adopted by nearly every maritime nation.[6] The United States Merchant Marine Academy, opened at King's Point in 1942, set the bar high for American licensed officers, and expanded through the 1970s. It was here that the crew of the nuclear-powered NS *Savannah* came for training prior to the unique cargo vessel's commissioning in 1962.[7]

Ship design saw an increased use of aluminum alloys in superstructures, and modular specialization that included RollOn/RollOff (RORO), Lighter-Aboard-Ship, and container technologies. During this era the last ships of the great transatlantic passenger fleet were constructed, including the fast SS *United States*, SS *France*, SS *Andrea Doria*, and another ten vessels for American, Italian, and Swedish lines. There was also gradual growth of the regional cruise ship fleets in the Mediterranean and Caribbean, even as passenger lines on both coasts and the Great Lakes succumbed to market pressures.

In the recreational marine, aluminum, fiberglass, carbon fiber, and nylon became commonplace in boats, sails, lines, and rigging, reducing maintenance and improving efficiency and safety. Personal watercraft like surfboards, jet skis, paddleboards, kayaks, and sailboards have all enjoyed periods of popularity.

Conclusion

To compare today's Merchant Marine with that of 1901 is an apples-to-oranges exercise, but illustrative nonetheless. Using the "List of Merchant Vessels of the United States" published by the US Treasury Department, and doing a rough tally on the 431 pages of listings, presents an interesting contrast with today's maritime situation in the United States.

At the turn of the twentieth century, there were about 14,800 merchant sailing ships registered in the country, large and small. Vessels powered by steam numbered near 8,640, about a quarter with iron or steel hulls, and about 8 percent over one thousand tons. There were about three thousand unrigged, unpowered barges of all descriptions. The navy had almost nine hundred commissioned craft, and over two hundred others were managed by other government entities like the Light House Establishment and the Fisheries Commission. Grand total: about 24,700 listed vessels.

Today, of course, the merchant sailing ship is gone, save for a few dozen research, museum, and training vessels. Steam vessels are rare; most commercial power plants are diesel-electric variations, and hulls are almost exclusively steel. According to the 2016 *World Factbook* published by the US Central Intelligence Agency, there were 393 US flagged ships registered in 2010; 18 percent were passenger carriers. By comparison, the top five countries—Panama, Liberia, China, Malta, and Hong Kong—had a combined total of 14,296 flagged vessels.[8]

The 2016 navy list shows 274 deployable ships, 21 percent on active duty—these numbers don't include the miscellaneous harbor craft listed in the 1901 roster. Five current enrollees are aircraft carriers supporting over 3,700 navy aircraft—just a dream in 1901. The Coast Guard maintains about two hundred large vessels, including cruisers, cutters, icebreakers, buoy tenders, and about four hundred small response craft. Rough total of significant ships on the US roster today: 850.[9]

These numbers are simply for comparison. The lists were created with varying criteria and the ships differ in myriad ways from each other. And there are government enforcement and scientific survey vessels, sponsored by individual states and municipalities, that aren't reflected here. If we throw in the millions of recreational craft that didn't exist in 1901, we certainly have more boats in the country than a century ago.

With the disappearance of millions of tons of commercial shipping, it is hard to deny that the US Merchant Marine has ceded a superior world ranking to a global market that moves ships at wages reminiscent of a century ago, still suffers from pirate activity, and costs international rescue enterprises billions of dollars. America, the largest economy in the world, ranks a distant twenty-sixth among merchant marines worldwide. For a nation that gets 95 percent of its goods by water, this seems like a serious strategic miscalculation. Despite declarations to this effect, neither governmental nor corporate interests seem concerned.

Notes

1. Bern Anderson, *By Sea and By River: The Naval History of the Civil War* (New York: Alfred A. Knopf, 1962), 8–9.

2. Anderson, *By Sea and By River*, 10–17, 43–47.

3. Joe Evangelista, Steward H. Wade, Caryln Swaim, and James P. Rife, *The History of the American Bureau of Shipping: 150th Anniversary* (Houston: ABS, 2013), 7. Accessed at http://ww2.eagle.org/content/dam/eagle/publications/2012/ABSHistory150.pdf.

4. Robert Fergus, ed., *Chicago River and Harbor Convention: An Account of Its Origins and Proceedings* (Chicago: Fergus Printing, 1882), 35.

5. Evangelista et al., *The History of the American Bureau of Shipping*, 49.

6. "Contribution of the International Maritime Organization (IMO) to the Secretary-General's Report on Oceans and the Law of the Sea, 2008," http://www.un.org/depts/los/consultative_process/mar_sec_submissions/imo.pdf.

7. Jeffrey Cruikshank and Chloe G. Kline, *In Peace and War: A History of the U.S. Merchant Marine Academy at Kings Point* (Hoboken, NJ: Wiley, 2008), 78–80, 187–96.

8. *World Factbook*, https://www.cia.gov/library/publications/the-world-factbook/rankorder/2108rank.html#us. Merchant marine compares all ships engaged in the carriage of goods; or all commercial vessels (as opposed to all nonmilitary ships), which excludes tugs, fishing vessels, offshore oil rigs, and the like.

9. http://www.navy.mil/navydata/nav_legacy.asp?id=146; according to the International Maritime Organization (IMO), there are more than fifty thousand merchant ships trading internationally in 2016, transporting every kind of cargo. The world fleet is registered in over 150 nations and manned by more than a million seafarers of virtually every nationality; http://www.imo.org/en/About/Events/WorldMaritimeDay/Pages/WMD-2016.aspx.

CHAPTER 3

BOATS AND SHIPS OF NORTH AMERICA

L IKE ANY tools, good boats and ships are ideally suited for their tasks. The demands of purpose and environment have been so refined over centuries that, between brutal commerce and Mother Nature, badly designed boats don't last long. Rowing shell, Roman trireme, super-tanker, fishing dory, skipjack—these types of vessels survived because they were good at what they did in the waters where they did it. To interpret boats or sailors, it's best to understand the vessels.

Vessels: Latin derivation, similar to "vase," although instead of holding water, they keep it out. Merriam-Webster places initial Anglo usage in the mid-fifteenth century, when shipbuilding in Western Europe began to blossom. By this time, regional rivals England, Spain, France, Belgium, Holland, Germany, and Russia were expanding their worldwide colonial reach into Asian, African, and eventually American territories. The markets they opened were profitable, prompting political and military expansion. Europeans invested vast amounts of capital to develop "vessels" that could carry cargo, armament, and personnel.

This prioritization of purpose reflects that of nearly every vessel built before and afterward: *physical properties* (buoyancy, construction style, material, propulsion, etc.) dictated by purpose and environment; *economic importance* (local, regional, national, international), as part of the continental transportation system; and *cultural legacy* (social influence, literature, world view), as an integral part of our heritage.

It should be noted that, while most North American maritime traditions discussed in this book are descended from those of Western Europe, Asian shipbuilding techniques, sea routes, and cultures were recorded as early as 2000 BCE. Much like seafaring industries on the eastern Mediterranean, ship production along the Indian Ocean, and later in waters off China, Korea, Japan, and Indonesia, catered to coastal trades. Vessels were generally shallow drafted and of modest size. Nonetheless, hull shape and motive power was sufficiently refined to permit sailors to explore the east African coast and across the Pacific Ocean as far as the Americas.

A vessel's primary purpose is to protect the crew, passengers, and cargo from surrounding water and weather. Secondarily, it should be fitted with some type of efficient propulsion system, and be shaped to maximize maneuverability. Tertiary considerations might include comfort, speed, and beauty. In most cases the process of developing the primary and secondary considerations satisfied the tertiary. A well-designed ship is seldom ugly or slow.

Visually and practically, the grace and beauty of ships can be powerful tools when presenting them in an exhibition or program. Full-scale representations of boats and ships—murals, models, cross-sections, or cradled boats—convey both the simplicity and complexity of hull construction and propulsion. Given appropriate space, the "lines" of a ship or the synchronous nature of a quadruple expansion steam engine can be appreciated at many levels. Replicas allow tactile experiences, and interactive possibilities are endless, including everything from whistle communication to hands-on boatbuilding.

Say What?

To better understand the development of vessels over the last several millennia, let us consider the many elements that go into ship—or boat—design.

First, what is the difference between a ship and a boat? A common reply is that a boat can fit on a ship, but a ship cannot fit on a boat. On the Great Lakes where vessels large and small are all called "boats," I find that this answer doesn't serve. In broad maritime parlance, "ship" can refer with equal correctness to *any* substantial vessel—hundred-foot schooner or thousand-foot freighter—or to a craft with a very specific arrangement of square-rigged sails. Ship can also refer to the process of "taking on," as in "we shipped a cargo," or "we shipped a lot of water" (meaning the boat was flooding). Ship is typical of a sailor's vocabulary: each word has a history and often multiple meanings. This text will employ vessel, ship, boat, craft, hull, and bottom to cover man-made things that float.

Many things on a boat have two names. The rudder used to be called a steering board, the etymology of "starboard," the side of a boat from which the steering board was suspended. "Port" was the other side—also called "larboard." "Port" is also a place where boats load and unload (also known as a harbor), or an opening in a hull (think "porthole"). Things called ropes by landfolk are known as lines on a boat. Cable refers to a way of making hemp rope, but now generally means a metal one. Lines can be halyards, rodes, sheets, guys, painters, lifts, and stays (stays can also be called shrouds). Similarly, spar is a word that refers to masts, booms, and poles. Steering devices are variously oars and rudders, manipulated by tillers, wheels, and whipstaffs. A floor can be a deck or a sole.

Within the construction of a vessel are a similar number of words not usually encountered ashore, most with ancient derivations. The term keel, the backbone of most vessels, derives from a Norwegian dialect and describes a foundation beam. Bow (pronounced like "wow") is also Nordic. Strake, garboard, and yacht are traceable to Dutch. Spar, for a pole, is found in old German and French. Mast is Anglo-Saxon with roots in the Roman era. Hull is Latin for shell. Anchor is Greek. Knee, referring to a supporting angle or beam, has roots in Sanskrit.[1]

From an interpretive standpoint, the difference between the lexicons of land and sea is an important "hook." Words can be a fun way to approach the nautical world; leeches and luffs, frapping and deadeyes, scuppers and baggy wrinkles are words most landsmen never encounter. Vocabulary takeaway fliers, parenthetical clarifications on didactic panels, or even specific (and possibly humorous) exhibits or workshops on "sailor talk" are all opportunities for interpretation. The language of the sea is different. Play with it.

How Does That Work?

More important than the language, it is imperative that guests finish their visit with at least an elementary understanding of the significance of hull shape and propulsion in relation to a vessel's purpose and usefulness.

This can be approached in many ways. Scientific principles can explain buoyancy, stability, and propulsion, and dovetails with many STEM-oriented curriculums. Economic and commercial perspectives help visitors understand why certain ship types were created and why they became the foundation of important commercial markets—or sometimes the markets were the foundation of the design. The easily understood chronological approach exposes visitors to the natural evolution of hull shapes and propulsion methods. Exhibits and presentations that track the development of technologies, markets, techniques, tools, and materials, all addressing particular environments and purposes, allow for smooth cognitive evolution within the visitor's mind.

A full explanation of shipbuilding cannot be accommodated in this chapter, and probably not in any but the rarest of exhibitions. There are a few key interpretive considerations that will serve here—and in your exhibits and programs—to help describe the evolution of vessels. They include *purpose, resources,* and *environment.*

Purpose, or need, drives all innovation, and boatbuilding is no different. "I must cross this river." "There are many fish to catch offshore." "This platform is well suited for my cannon." "I need to go faster than that fellow." Purpose describes what a vessel must be able to accomplish; it is the key question when developing any craft, be it a yacht, battleship, or dredge.

Resources are almost as important, as they define the type of boat that can be built. In a place with abundant trees, a log makes a fine "boat," straddled by its pilot and paddled with a stick—adventurous, no craftsmanship necessary. Where sinew, roots, and vines are available, rafts are practicable. Banded wood or reed provides an easily built, stable, and effective platform; better in protected waterways, but with open water history, too. With the development of bone and copper tools, dugout canoes, bark boats, and skin boats became options in forested areas—lighter, more manageable, capable of carrying more people and goods. Iron tools—including knives, axes, adzes, mauls, chisels, and saws—allowed wooden beams and boards to be crafted into elaborate frameworks.

Vessels are generally composed of a skeleton with sheathing. Perhaps the simplest demonstration of a viable vessel framework is a leaf from an elm or poplar tree (many species will suffice). Once it has dried and fallen, the leaf often shrinks into the shape representing a very viable craft. It has a prow—called the "stem" on both a leaf and a boat—an integrated keel, frames, and sheathing. One can place a leaf in a bowl of water

Figure 3.1 This leaf has all the elements of a good boat: a central spine or keel, radiating skeleton or ribs, and a waterproof sheathing. This efficient shape was copied by the Egyptians (c. 2600 BCE) and Vikings (c. 900).

and gradually pour in sand to demonstrate how skin and frame technology can carry a lot of cargo. The leaf, which weighs grams, can support several times its weight in sand. Early boatbuilders understood this and emulated it.

The shape of each boat is influenced by purpose and environment, but dictated by available resources—bone, wood, hide, canvas, cordage, iron, steel, tar, epoxy, carbon fiber. Environment traditionally dictates resource availability, and has an equally important influence on a boat's purpose and design requirements. For instance, skin vessels built in the arctic place a premium on the use of wooden supports, resulting in a light and resilient shell. Boats operating on generally waveless rivers feature open decks close to the water and shallow hulls. Those created for running river rapids and swift currents are light but strong and agile. Open-water vessels—sail or steam—have solid hulls, high sides, and watertight hatches.

Construction techniques and tools are great ways to take visitors and students to the second level; beyond the what, to the how and why, and the myriad ways that various cultures adapted various concepts. Such presentations can be passive, using full-scale cross-sections, models, and drawings. Or they can involve interactive activities that demonstrate framing, rigging, loading, or driving a boat.

Beyond the vessels, models and dioramas are effective ways to illustrate auxiliary maritime structures, such as dry docks, locks, lighthouses, caissons, dockyards, and waterfront neighborhoods. Dry docks are ship-sized chambers from which the water can be pumped, allowing a craft's hull to be exposed for inspection or repair—artificial "holes in the water." Locks are chambers that allow ships to pass between bodies of water that are at different levels, often the intermediary route around waterfalls or rapids. Lighthouses, in many forms, can be substantial and innovative assemblies, particularly if they are constructed offshore. Caissons are also "holes in the water" that allow underwater construction of bridge piers and locks. Together, these are engineering marvels of the North American maritime, and fixtures in shipyards and waterfronts.

What Makes It Go?

Propulsion is a commonality shared by all vessels. To attend to their assigned purposes, boats need to move efficiently from point A to point B. Tools used to propel various craft can be as simple as a carved stick—a paddle—or as complicated as water jets. With a history as rich as hull development, and a lexicon as complicated and unfamiliar, propulsion can be equally daunting. However, broken down into three categories—*human-powered, wind-powered,* and *machine-powered*—it becomes easier to understand.

Today, human-powered boats in North America include kayaks, canoes, and rowing shells, all based on ancient forms of propulsion. Paddled boats used for hunting, harvesting, and trade—umiaks, kayaks, and canoes—predate written records. Rowing is likely as ancient and was used primarily in a commercial or military capacity. The major trading vessels of the North Atlantic, Mediterranean, and Asia were rowed, often by slaves, with auxiliary sail power. Galleys of the Phoenicians, Egyptians, and ancient Greeks and Romans often carried three hundred rowers, and served the commercial and military needs of their owners. On a smaller scale, Viking longboats depended on both oars and sail. The American whaleboat employed sail to pursue a fish, but relied on a half-dozen spirited oarsmen to close the target, and then tow the dead whale back to the factory ship. American oarsmen have served fishing dories, cargo lighters, river ferries, and barges.

Sails, used to harness wind energy, are nearly as ancient as paddles and oars. Wind, however, can be fickle, so sails were generally auxiliary propulsion. There were small, ancient fishing and trading vessels with efficient rigs that relied on sails for primary power, but it wasn't until improvements in sail- and rope-making in the fifteenth century that large ships became simply "sailing ships." The Spanish and Portuguese developed vessels for exploration and commerce that were quickly emulated by the major kingdoms of northern Europe. By the nineteenth century—the Great Age of Sail—rigging platforms included dozens of efficient configurations, ranging from simple sloops and schooners, to highly refined, multimasted arrays capable of carrying dozens of sails at a time. Sail remained viable through the first few decades of the twentieth century, simply because fuel was free and labor costs low. Today, sailing exists only in the realm of recreation and competition, but this in itself represents a significant history. Once the purview of the wealthy, today recreational sailing can be enjoyed by nearly everyone interested in the sport.

Mechanical propulsion is a relatively recent development. The practical application of steam to move hulls was dependent upon engineering and metallurgical developments that created reliable boilers, engine blocks, shafts, and rods. By the late eighteenth century, steam engines were becoming a reliable but unproven tool. Among North American innovators leveraging British technology were three unfamiliar progenitors—William Henry, James Rumsey, John Fitch—and two familiar patentholders—Robert Fulton and Robert Livingston. Reliable steamboats, utilizing side-mounted paddles, established regular passenger services on rivers of the East Coast soon after the American Revolutionary War was over. Steamboat service was inaugurated in 1811 on the Ohio River of the western rivers system, in 1817 on Lake Ontario, and the following year on the upper Great Lakes.

Paddlewheels, either side-mounted or stern-mounted, remained commercially viable through the nineteenth century, but paddles were gradually replaced by propellers, a trend starting prior to the American Civil War. Though initially slower by about a third, propeller-powered vessels used half the fuel, historically wood, coal, and then oil. They were simpler systems, and occupied less of the hold of the ship. Steam has given way to diesel-generated electric propulsion systems for most of the world's commercial marine applications, but even nuclear fission systems aboard icebreakers and submarines are steam-generating electrical power plants.

From an interpretive standpoint, two-story tall quadruple expansion steam engines are awe-inspiring; museums grab visitors simply by displaying them and explaining them. One of my favorite museums has their engine operational and—better yet—controlled from a touch pad by visitors.

But that's not the end of the story. Windmills have successfully powered propeller vessels into the wind. Horses have powered paddled ferries. Naphtha, and later gasoline, became common fuels for motors in recreational boats. Nuclear fuels, biofuels (nonwood or coal), and solar fuels all have viability. As of this writing, boats can be purchased that are driven by exercise-like machines with bicycle, coffee-grinder, or stair-stepper action, allowing people of any capability to make a boat go. There can be fun in propulsion.

In North America, most forms of historic propulsion have practitioners and proponents. Gatherings of steam engine aficionados occur across the continent, and marine engines and motors are well represented. Classic schooners offer excursions and training. Museums can partner with local rowing clubs to present regattas, and with yacht clubs for sailing opportunities and outreach. Affinity organizations like the Antique Outboard Motor Club, modeling groups, or antique wooden boat owners can make great partners for onsite presentations and events.

From Christening to Grave

Biography is a powerful opportunity for interpretation. Notably, in the maritime world, biography includes the lives of both humans and vessels. People are the heart of most historical narratives, providing records, context, and color. In the maritime world, vessels are similarly credited with distinct traits, personalities, and documented lifespans.

The human participants in North America's maritime comprise a wide swath of social and cultural strata, from the wealthiest to the most destitute. At the top are investors, including bankers, shareholders, licensed officers, and shipping agents. At the bottom are common sailors, a classification comprised of smart, athletic, inventive people who may also be slaves, debtors, criminals, and society's rejects. In the middle are masters, officers, and government agents whose state in the marine world is distinctly middle class. All live under a very strict hierarchy, creating a social dynamic unlike anything elsewhere.

Their stories—particularly local ones—can be excellent touchpoints for an exhibit, lesson plan, or presentation. Physical material and artifacts are commonly used tools and can be powerful. Interpretive opportunities exist if the biography's subject has been historically vilified or canonized; generally the better story is somewhere in between, but should be approached cautiously. Similar caution if the subject's descendants are involved in the presentation development process.

Arguably the more common biographies are those of the vessels themselves. Historically, the sailing community has personified them with deference, assigning them a female gender. Vessels are almost universally referred to by mariners as "she" and "her," perhaps recognizing a dependence upon the vessel which bears them, or a personal relationship which people develop for their homes, farms, pets, and cars. So many narratives include passages akin to, "The ship fought valiantly through the storm," personifying its strength, but also its bravery. In many harbors, even nonsailing folk watch ships come and go, aware of the individual vessel names, and often knowledgeable about captains, cargoes, and destinations.

Museum interpretation has long embraced vessel biographies. Indeed, entire institutions have been created to tell the story of a single vessel. More often, the life of a ship is woven into a related exhibition storyline—a storm, a battle, an industry. From a research standpoint, if we equate ship plans and construction contracts to baby pictures and birth certificates, the available record for most ships offers information from conception and christening to death and burial—often with lots of pictures. Much like a human's biography, the record prioritizes physical dimensions, build, and coloring, but also explores heroic feats, record-breaking voyages, harrowing encounters, accidents, repairs, peccadillos, and quirks.

In the case of shipwreck interpretation, biographies are intimately told; the vessel's life intertwined with the lives of the crew and passengers. Good interpretation must carefully balance human tragedy with the craft's tragedy. Understandably, a ship's final moments are vital to understanding why a reliable hull succumbed to the sea, and how humans reacted—heroically or not so. Care should be taken when deciding editorial emphasis. Empathy is an important emotion that can be overwhelmed.

Vessel records—ship plans, custom records, legal claims, press clippings—are available in both public and private venues, from the National Archives to small local repositories.

Conclusion

Interpreting vessels is easy, once you get beyond the unfamiliar lexicon and environment. Start with, "What is its purpose?" Purpose defines design and skills: What does it carry? How big is it? How is it propelled? What is it made of? What is the shape? How big is the crew? How do they live? Anticipate the obvious questions: Why do they float? Why does it look like that? Where do you go to the bathroom?

There are great opportunities for interpretation by simply exposing people to boats.

Note

1. Ernest Weekley, *An Etymological Dictionary of Modern English* (New York: Dover Publications, 1967).

PART II

Case Studies

CHAPTER 4

LAYERS OF INTERPRETATION

The *Charles W. Morgan*'s Changing Role at Mystic Seaport

Erik Ingmundson

THE MORNING of November 8, 1941 was a typically cold, gray, late autumn day on the Connecticut coast. In just one month, the United States and Great Britain would declare war on the empire of Japan. While concerns about the war were undoubtedly on many people's minds, the residents of Stonington and Groton, Connecticut, greeted the morning with excitement. The two towns stand on opposite shores of the Mystic River, a tidal estuary winding some three and a half miles inland from Long Island Sound. In just a matter of hours, the *Charles W. Morgan*, a whaleship built one hundred years before, was due to arrive at the mouth of the Mystic River. A small maritime museum, then called the Marine Historical Association (which would become Mystic Seaport) had acquired the vessel, hoping to make it the centerpiece of a growing collection.

Joseph Gordon, a high school biology teacher from Stonington, wanted to catch a glimpse of the *Morgan* during her transit. He joined a friend aboard a motorboat, and together, they made their way to the mouth of the Mystic River. There, Gordon recalled, "looming larger and clearer, was the *Morgan*, her bare masts and strangely angled spars stark against the sky. Like a *Flying Dutchman*, the whaler was without visible sign of power as she crested the gray waters speeding to her new home."[1] Gordon convinced his friend to position their boat alongside the old whaler. With cameras in hand, he climbed aboard. Captain William Henry Tripp greeted him warmly and invited him to remain aboard to document the final phase of the *Morgan*'s transit upriver.

Figure 4.1 The *Charles W. Morgan* under tow, 1941. Image courtesy of Mystic Seaport.

Despite the calm conditions, the trip was not without difficulty. The *Morgan* was leaking badly, and a bilge pump ran constantly to keep her afloat.[2] She touched the bottom twice. At last, Captain Tripp brought her to rest at a mooring on the river's eastern shore. After thirty-seven voyages, the *Morgan*'s life as an active whaler was over, and her life as a museum artifact began. For over seventy years, she stayed at Mystic Seaport. Then, in 2014, a remarkable event happened. She went back to sea.

Even if an artifact is protected with the utmost of care, it is not immune to change. In watercraft preservation, this is certainly true on a material level. Indeed, the *Charles W. Morgan* has undergone multiple restorations to remain afloat. Today, less than 15 percent of her structure is original to 1841. Beyond the confines of material, though, is another dynamic process of change—the relationship that we as humans have with the artifact. As Susan Pearce notes, artifacts play a key role in how "we construct our ever-passing present."[3] Interpretations of the past are always shaped by present and future concerns.

This case study aims to trace the *Charles W. Morgan*'s evolution as a living artifact in the context of broader changes that have shaped the theory and practice of history museums during the past seventy-five years. By doing so, I hope to assist other museum professionals in developing a more nuanced understanding of how our field has changed over time.

The traditional narrative arc of the museum profession describes a paradigm shift in priorities. Early museums were focused heavily on collecting and preserving artifacts. More recently museums have focused their energies on "providing a variety of primarily educational services to the public."[4] There is plenty of evidence to support this view. Yet museum professionals can fall into the trap of describing this evolution in strictly binary terms (the "old way" versus the "new way"). A better approach is to think of museums as adding *layers* of understanding over time. Each generation charts some new courses, but also builds on the work of its predecessors. In our quest to make our work relevant to twenty-first-century audiences, today's public historians would do well to look back while also looking ahead. The history of Mystic Seaport's interpretation of the *Charles W. Morgan* illustrates this clearly.

Background

The *Charles W. Morgan* was built in 1841 by the Hillman Brothers shipyard of New Bedford, Massachusetts. The vessel has an overall length of 133 feet, a beam of 27.7 feet, and a gross register tonnage of 313.75. She is the last surviving example of some 2,700 wooden whaling ships that once traveled the world's oceans. She was an active American whaler for eighty years, a remarkable feat considering that most comparable vessels seldom lasted more than twenty. After her whaling days ended, she spent several years sitting idly in New Bedford. Eventually, the vessel was moved to the estate of Edward Howland Robinson Green, the son of Henrietta "Hetty" Green, the infamous "Witch of Wall Street." Green had the vessel placed in a sand berth, and permitted public access until his death in 1935. Unfortunately, Green left no money or provision for its stewardship in his will, so the Marine Historical Association ultimately acquired the *Morgan* in 1941. This institution ultimately became Mystic Seaport, with the *Charles W. Morgan* as its flagship.[5]

Layer I: A Bulwark of Democracy, 1941–1960

During the time when the *Charles W. Morgan* came to Mystic in 1941, some were raising questions about the museum field's direction. The trauma of the Great Depression and the onset of World War II led some to view museums as a crucial bulwark against domestic and foreign threats. For Theodore Low, an educator at the Metropolitan Museum of Art in 1942, every museum had "a distinct moral duty to the community in which [it was] situated." He denounced an emphasis on acquisition and preservation that marginalized public education as "a necessary but isolated evil." The duty to educate, he argued, encompassed "all types and all classes of people."[6] This egalitarian duty was coequal to another responsibility—"to play an exceedingly important role in maintaining and strengthening that thing which we like to call 'The American Way of Life.'"[7] For Low, the museum was no vault for curios acquired by a privileged class. Rather, it was a vital social and political institution that could uphold democratic values in a time of crisis.

The Marine Historical Association framed the acquisition of the *Charles W. Morgan* in a very similar manner. In a 1942 pamphlet titled *Why the "Morgan" Came to Mystic*, the vessel was portrayed as something that could "signify for coming generations that vigorous root of Americanism known as 'New England Character.'" Its arrival was "an important indication of the revival of American maritime supremacy." The vessel's preservation and interpretation would inspire a "living interest in the sea, and the development of those sturdy traits which [would] regain for America her reputation on the seven seas." This message of patriotism was accompanied by a strong democratic ethos. The *Morgan* (along with the rest of the museum's growing collection), belonged "not to the few who [had] sponsored it, but to every American who [felt] the surge of seafaring ancestry within his veins." For the Marine Historical Association's founding members Dr. Charles K. Stillman, Edward Bradley, and Carl C. Cutler, acquiring artifacts like the *Charles W. Morgan* was not an end to itself. They, like Theodore Low, saw in their work a much larger, intangible purpose.

With the benefit of chronological distance, we can also see some of this vision's limitations. In this period of the *Morgan*'s life at Mystic Seaport, the visiting public was expected to understand the vessel's history in collective, monolithic terms. Such an approach mirrored that being taken by academic historians called "consensus history." Adherents to this approach—such as Daniel Boorstin and Richard Hofstadter—tended to minimize the role of conflicts in their interpretations of the past, presenting American history as a narrative of continual progress.[8] We can see elements of this consensus narrative in Mystic Seaport's early presentation of itself. The pamphlet referenced earlier speaks of the common traits of "New England character." This unifying impulse negated the personal, individual experiences between visitors and artifacts.

To be fair, the museum's staff was not completely oblivious to the process of individual meaning-making. In fact, hints of this process can be seen in the museum's early printed materials. In a guide for visitors published in 1952 (which featured an image of the *Morgan* on its cover), Assistant Curator MacDonald Steers described the guidebook as "a running series of comments, with no particular effort to give priority to the more important items; for who, but you, shall be the judge of that?" Yes, there was room for individual experiences with objects. However, the nature of the museum's approach was to keep these experiences private. Of greater importance was a belief that the *Morgan* was imbued with an inherent message that the visitor needed to understand. When Freeman Tilden published his seminal work, *Interpreting Our Heritage* in 1957, he called for a more personalized learning process that would place a greater emphasis on the visitor's own interests. That process was undoubtedly happening privately at Mystic Seaport, but not so much publicly. However, it was a harbinger of an idea that would drive the thirty-eighth voyage over sixty years later.

Layer II: An Interest in Technology and Experiential Learning, 1960–1975

As the *Morgan* settled into its third decade of life as a museum exhibit, its interpretation became narrower in scope. The sweeping proclamations about America's return to global supremacy receded slightly. Instead, a greater emphasis was placed on the ship itself and all of the objects associated with it. Andrew German, a longtime editor of Mystic Seaport's publications, saw this change as a partial result of the tremendous growth of technology during this period. "In the 1960s," he recalled, "as the nation challenged space, it was the epic struggle of man and whale that captured the visitor's imagination."[9] Mystic Seaport's Executive Vice President Susan Funk described this period as "the *Popular Mechanics*" approach to interpreting the vessel. The refinement of whale craft (whale hunting tools), the evolution of whaleboat design, and the growth of whaling from a small shore-based industry to one that touched all of the world's oceans figured prominently in the vessel's presentation to the public.[10]

The greater focus on the ship itself can also be explained by a practical reality of the time—the museum's staff members were getting to know the vessel better. From 1953 to 1963, a small number of museum staff had done piecemeal restoration work on the vessel.[11] The work was largely cosmetic in nature, and the vessel was not afloat, but permanently berthed in sand and mud by the river's edge. By 1968, the vessel had been designated a National Historic Landmark, but Curator Edmund P. Lynch feared the *Morgan* was on borrowed time. In a memorandum to the institution's board, he argued passionately that the museum needed to invest in the necessary infrastructure improvements to allow the vessel to float once again. "If we are so short of funds that we cannot maintain a National Landmark," he charged, "then the most conclusive evaluation ever undertaken by this Association must begin now."[12] The board responded to his call for action, and the construction of a preservation shipyard facility and lift dock on the southern end of the museum's property began in 1970. On December 6, the *Morgan* was freed from her sand berth and floated into the river.[13] In a sense, because of her return to the water, she was more "alive" than she had been in years. By investing in a preservation shipyard, Mystic Seaport sought not just to preserve the *Morgan* itself, but also the skills of the many generations of shipwrights that had built and maintained her.

The *Morgan*'s return to the water also coincided with a growing interest among history professionals in the study of material culture. E. McClung Fleming published his model for artifact study in 1974, which challenged cultural historians to look beyond traditional documentary sources.[14] Historian of agriculture John T. Schlebecker went a step further when he suggested, "if at all possible the object should be touched, handled, and lifted."[15] A proponent of tactile learning, he noted that "actually trying out some tool, or replica, opens new insights because it is possible to discover how a tool was actually used."[16] Thus, we can also see how this growing interest in the *Morgan* as an object of study dovetailed with broader trends in the public and academic history communities.

This desire to not just observe artifacts, but reanimate them, played a role in the growth of the museum's programmatic offerings. Beginning in the summer of 1972, Mystic Seaport established a new form of ensemble interpretation called the "Demonstration Squad." Teams of six interpreters climbed aloft on the *Morgan* to show how big square sails were set and furled. They rowed whaleboats out into the river and demonstrated various maneuvers twice a day, and even sailed a whaleboat on occasion. To coordinate their work, they incorporated classic working "chanteys" into their demonstrations, and also held formal sea music performances several times per day. The visitor experience itself, though, did not include much in the way of learning conversations with the general public. As was the case in earlier years, the visitor-artifact connections were more private than publicly celebrated and acknowledged. Also, the intense focus on the material aspects of the ship and its history tended to homogenize the human aspects of the vessel's history. This would change in the years to come.

Layer III: Sharing New Stories: The Influence of Social History and Cultural Analysis, 1975–2008

By the mid-1960s, "consensus history" was falling into disfavor in academic circles. The issues of civil rights, women's rights, and the antiwar movement (among others) began driving historians to share the stories of groups that had been marginalized, "oppressed and dispossessed." This scholarly movement came to be known as the "*new* social history," and gained traction in the decades that followed.[17] It preferred "pluralism to homogeneity, conflict to consensus."[18] Complementing this was another shift known as the "cultural turn." Following the publication of anthropologist Clifford Geertz's *The Interpretation of Cultures* in 1973, some historians began drawing on literature, visual art, dance, music, and other such cultural symbols as part of a larger system of shared meanings and ideas.[19]

These currents pushed Mystic Seaport's interpretation of the *Morgan* in different directions, albeit gradually. The explanation for this incrementalism is both philosophical and practical. As Daniel Vickers noted in 1993, academic history paid "little heed" to maritime subject matter.[20] Also, social history and cultural history were both nascent fields in American academic circles, and it took time for new generations of history practitioners to absorb their training and start putting it to use. Eventually, though, these changes started making inroads. Marginalized voices started to be heard, and the *Morgan* came to be understood not just as a physical artifact, but as a cultural nexus. In 1980, Mystic Seaport organized its first Sea Music Festival and Symposium. Seaport staff members Geoff Kaufman and Craig Edwards imbued the event with a multicultural understanding of maritime folk music grounded in ethnomusicology. That tradition continues to this day, and music is frequently used as a tool for highlighting the *Morgan*'s multicultural dimensions.[21]

Beginning in the 1990s and into the first decade of the new millennium, the social and cultural seeds sown in earlier years came into full bloom. In 1991, as the *Morgan* turned 150 years old, seaport historian Andrew German remarked that,

> Now, in view of the nation's ethnic diversity and search for roots, we look to the ship-board world of the mariner and the many peoples—Native American, New England Yankee, Virginian, Scandinavian, West Indian, Cape Verdean, Hawaiian, Samoan, Japanese, Philippine—who have lived in the *Morgan*'s forecastle, stood at her wheel, and risked their lives in her whaleboats.[22]

This change of focus manifested itself in numerous ways. In 1995, a conference focused on "Race, Ethnicity, and Power in Maritime America" was held at Mystic Seaport.

Between 1998 and 2000, the Freedom Schooner *Amistad* was constructed in the museum's shipyard. There was also a veritable explosion of maritime scholarship imbued with social and cultural perspectives, including Joan Druett's *Petticoat Whalers* (1991), Briton Cooper Busch's *Whaling Will Never Do for Me: The American Whaleman of the Nineteenth Century* (1994), W. Jeffrey Bolster's *Black Jacks: African American Seamen in the Age of Sail* (1997), Lisa Norling's *Captain Ahab Had a Wife* (2000), and Hester Blum's *The View from the Masthead: Maritime Imagination and Antebellum American Sea Narratives* (2008), among others. At Mystic Seaport, exhibits focused on immigration, women's history, African American sailors, and cross-cultural exchanges with Inuit peoples provided a far more diverse environment for interpreting the *Morgan* than there had ever been before.

Despite these tremendous efforts, by 2008, Mystic Seaport and the broader museum community had to face some harsh realities. The National Endowment for the Arts reported that attendance at art and cultural institutions was "at a glance, disappointing."[23] A growing amount of audience research showed (and continues to show) that history museum visitors are increasingly older and less racially or ethnically diverse than the majority of the nation's population.[24] The global economic downturn of 2007–2008 forced Mystic Seaport to drastically tighten its belt, and prompted some hard questions. Despite a whole host of efforts to tell more inclusive stories, the data showed that fewer visitors were coming. By 2008, the *Morgan* needed extensive restoration work. Faced with these challenges, the staff of Mystic Seaport would push themselves to make the *Morgan*'s story relevant to the twenty-first-century public.

Layer IV: A Journey of Shared Experiences: 2008–2015

Mystic Seaport's management team knew that the *Morgan* was due for an extensive restoration. Outgoing Mystic Seaport President Douglas Teeson challenged the museum's staff to do the restoration work "famously." From there, incoming President Steven C. White dared to raise a once unthinkable question—could the museum's staff imagine sailing the vessel again? For years, the staff had routinely told the public that the vessel would *never* sail again. Why would any institution allow its most famous and iconic artifact to venture out into the (literal and figurative) "wild blue yonder"? Yet, as White continued to pose these questions, he found that a growing number of staff, trustees, and members were beginning to think differently. Once the restoration work was complete, the vessel would be in excellent condition. Furthermore, a small part of the *Morgan*'s structure was still original to 1841. The idea of sailing the vessel when she had some of her original "bones" intact was compelling.

During a series of internal meetings, the museum's board and senior management team agreed on some nonnegotiable principles to frame the work ahead. The first was that sailing the vessel could not, in any way, compromise the integrity of the artifact in the long term. Fitting the vessel with engines and extra thru-hull fittings was deemed unacceptable. A second key principle was that the voyage could not simply happen for the sake of itself. Instead, it needed, as Susan Funk put it, "to add something to the historical

Figure 4.2 The *Charles W. Morgan* is permanently moored at Mystic Seaport in Mystic, Connecticut, adjoining the historic village and a variety of other vessels. Photograph by Carol M. Highsmith. Courtesy of the Library of Congress.

record," both in the museum's collections, and in the broader public history community. In 2009, the Board of Trustees officially announced that the *Morgan* would sail again.

While there was considerable excitement about this project within the museum's ranks, the staff also had very real concerns about sharing it with the public in a way that would engage rather than alienate. Discussing the brutal realities of commercial whale hunting in a world more accustomed to whale *watching* was difficult, and posed a major obstacle for fundraising. In January 2012, the museum convened a charrette of maritime historians, scientists, and museum professionals. This feedback (along with many staff meetings) led to the development of four core themes that would guide the entire project.[25] They were articulated in an application for a Chairman's level grant from the National Endowment for the Humanities (the NEH ultimately awarded Mystic Seaport $450,000). The themes were as follows:

1. "Changing perceptions of an acceptable stance toward whales and whaling show a dramatic shift in American understanding of humans' place in the natural world since the *Morgan*'s whaling days."
2. "The American whale fishery was a volatile, high-risk, and high-profit industry."
3. "Whaling ships were cultural crossroads, placing men of many different racial, ethnic, and cultural backgrounds in a small space for long stretches of time."
4. "Whaling has had, and continues to have, a significant impact on American culture."

Interpretive themes can serve as a practical tool for keeping programs focused, and can prevent a visitor's mind from becoming lost in factual minutia.[26] In the case of the thirty-eighth voyage, they also were crucial in helping partner organizations see how they fit into the project. The National Oceanic and Atmospheric Administration (NOAA) saw the voyage as an opportunity to showcase their efforts to preserve habitats for whales and other marine life, and to place their work in a broader historical context. When the *Morgan* sailed among humpback whales on Stellwagen Bank National Marine Sanctuary, NOAA provided a support vessel, and also streamed live broadcasts called "Oceans Live." They also provided staff and informational displays at every port the *Morgan* visited. NOAA's involvement brought a greater amount of depth and nuance to the first theme than Mystic Seaport could have provided alone.

The themes also allowed each port to use the *Morgan* as a focal point for telling a stronger, place-based story about their own past. Some had direct connections to the vessel, while others were more general. The New Bedford Whaling Museum (and a host of other local organizations) presented the *Morgan*'s return to New Bedford as a big "homecoming party." For Martha's Vineyard, the *Morgan*'s return brought back long-dormant memories of islanders who had sailed the world's oceans aboard her, and drew greater attention to the island's history prior to becoming a resort community.[27] When the *Morgan* docked alongside the USS *Constitution* in Boston, its presence highlighted the role that "Old Ironsides" played in the protection and expansion of American maritime commerce. For

Figure 4.3 While on its historic tour, a whaleboat of the *Charles W. Morgan* conducted crew demonstrations and engaged with local whales in a manner far different than a century ago. Photograph by Andy Price. Courtesy of Mystic Seaport.

Newport, Rhode Island, the *Morgan* signified the region's earlier connections to whaling prior to its growth as a hub for naval activities and recreational yachting. Finally, the *Morgan*'s visit to the Massachusetts Maritime Academy highlighted the nation's history as a maritime power, and also drew greater attention to the centennial celebration of the Cape Cod Canal.

At each port of call, Mystic Seaport's staff organized a variety of educational activities in the dockside areas. The ship itself was of course a huge attraction, and because of the large crowds and capacity limits museum staff and volunteers were not in a position to have extended learning conversations with visitors on board. Instead, this portion of the experience involved walking the length of the vessel below decks, friendly (albeit quick) interactions with staff and crew, and enjoying the opportunity to see the vessel up close. The dockside programs featured sea music performances, theatrical programs (including an original work called *Moby-Dick in Minutes*), nineteenth-century costumed role-players, demonstrations of historic trades associated with seaport towns (such as blacksmithing, rope making, and coopering), demonstrations of whaleboat maneuvers, and opportunities for visitors to try rowing a whaleboat themselves. Taken together, these activities highlighted the economic and cultural impact of American whaling, provided active learning opportunities, and showcased the museum's strongest programmatic offerings in a setting outside of its Connecticut campus. During the course of the voyage, over sixty thousand people visited the *Morgan* in its various ports of call. That being said, simply taking Mystic Seaport "on the road" was not sufficient. If the museum was to meet the goal of adding something of value to the historical record, then some other approaches were necessary. To that end, two other projects were conceived—the *38th*

Voyagers project, and the *Morgan Stowaway*. Both were supported entirely by funding from the NEH grant.

These projects were also inspired by a combination of theoretical and practical ideas that have recently gained more traction in the broader museum community. The first, which museum learning theorist George Hein advocates, is the idea that museum visitors do not passively absorb ideas, but instead construct meaning by synthesizing learning experiences with previously learned knowledge, values, and beliefs.[28] Researchers John Falk and Lynn Dierking have argued that "All learning is a cumulative, long-term process, a process of making meaning and finding connections."[29] Another key concept is one that Sam H. Ham calls "the zone of tolerance." He argues that interpretive programs can be oriented toward different levels of engagement, including the "unrestricted zone" in which visitors simply think about a theme, the "wide zone" in which visitors construct individual meanings with an "appreciative point of view," and finally the "narrow zone" in which visitors retain a very specific thematic message.[30] On the practitioner's side, Nina Simon is widely credited as taking these theoretical concepts and showing how they can be applied to create what she calls "participatory" learning experiences in which "visitors can create, share, and connect with each other around content."[31]

The *38th Voyagers* project was managed in a manner similar to a conference or symposium. The museum sent out a call for proposals with the tagline "Go to sea aboard an historic tall ship, then tell your tale to the world." Each participant would have an opportunity to spend one night sleeping in a bunk aboard the vessel, and go sailing aboard the *Morgan* on the following day. They were expected to use their own talents to document and share the experience with others, with the goal of "producing finished products for the museum to share online and through exhibits, publications, and public programs." The vessel's limited passenger capacity necessitated a highly selective process. Out of two hundred eighty-four submissions, eighty-five were accepted. The final cohort included journalists, writers, educators, artists, humanities scholars, and scientists.[32] They were given up to a year to let the experience incubate in their minds and generate the project envisioned in their proposals. Throughout the process, the museum gave the voyagers enough space to interpret the vessel within the context of their own interests and work. At the same time, the museum chose applicants whose work would fall into Ham's "wide zone" of tolerance, resulting in projects that were diverse, yet rooted in a respectful (though not unquestioning) point of view. Many of their projects can be accessed via a digital exhibition (http://www.mysticseaport.org/voyage/voyagers/).

The *Stowaway* project was slightly different, as it entailed hiring someone to live aboard the vessel for the entire voyage's duration. Drawing inspiration from a project at Chicago's Museum of Science and Industry called "Month at the Museum," the Stowaway was tasked with immersing themselves in the experience of sailing aboard the *Morgan* and sharing it with the public via social media outlets (Instagram, Twitter, YouTube, and Facebook) and a blog on the museum's website. Applicants were asked to submit a written application, samples of their work, and a sixty-second video in which they highlighted their strengths as an applicant. The museum collaborated with a marketing firm to promote the project around the country. Ten finalist videos were posted on

38TH VOYAGE STOWAWAY

After reviewing scores of applications and video auditions from qualified candidates, Mystic Seaport has selected journalist Ryan Leighton, of Boothbay, Maine, to stow away aboard the *Charles W. Morgan*, America's oldest surviving merchant vessel, during her 38th Voyage this summer.

As the stowaway, Leighton will be immersed in all aspects of the 19th-century whaleship's 38th Voyage — living on board the ship with the crew, handling the sails and lines, steering the ship, and most important, sharing his daily experiences through a blog and social media platforms.

"Ryan proved he has the 'sense of the adventure' Mystic Seaport was searching for from the outset of the stowaway contest," said Susan Funk, executive vice president of Mystic Seaport. "As a successful journalist, he has relevant experience and the necessary skills to fulfill the role of the stowaway aboard the *Morgan's* most documented voyage ever. In addition to his enthusiasm, we are confident Ryan will bring his tireless work ethic, his ability to adapt to new situations, and his creativity to the 38th Voyage."

Leighton, who graduated from the University of Maine

Follow the Stowaway's Journey

- Blog: www.mysticseaport.org/stowaway
- Twitter: @MorganStowaway @MysticSeaport
- Facebook: www.facebook.com/mysticseaport
- The 38th Voyage

National Endowment for the Humanities

The Stowaway program has been made possible in part by a major grant from the National Endowment for the Humanities: Exploring the human endeavor. Any views, findings, conclusions, or recommendations expressed in this program do not necessarily represent those of the National Endowment for the Humanities.

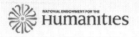

Figure 4.4 Ryan Leighton was selected "Stowaway" for the thirty-eighth voyage, and provided a regular narrative for audiences on the internet and various social media. Screenshot of http://www.mysticseaport.org/38thvoyage/stowaway10/.

Mystic Seaport's Facebook page, and users were encouraged to "like" their favorite videos (though this did not determine the final selection). The museum ultimately hired Ryan Leighton, a journalist and aspiring filmmaker from Boothbay Harbor, Maine, for the job.

Throughout the summer, Leighton chronicled his experiences in real time through a combination of blog posts, digital photos, and short videos. His work had two principal foci—describing the experience of sailing aboard the vessel (though comfortable around boats, he had no significant prior sailing experience), and providing a forum for visitors to share their perspectives with a broader audience. His most popular example of describing shipboard life involved strapping a GoPro camera to deckhand Cassie Sleeper, which she wore while climbing all the way to the royal yard on the mainmast—the highest point a crew member could climb aloft. The video has been viewed on YouTube over 153,000 times, and garnered comments such as "I'm pretty terrified of heights, but that view is amazing," and "Sweaty palms looking at it." For showcasing the vessel's significance to individuals, Leighton's strongest piece of work was a video titled "Stowie's Street Cam," which he shot in New Bedford. The video was a collection of various interviews with visitors in which he asked them to articulate why the *Morgan* was significant to them personally. All of Ryan's work is exhibited online at http://www.mysticseaport.org/38thvoyage/stowaway10/.

In sum, the *38th Voyage* represented the culmination of the interpretive layers that have been described previously. Layer one can be seen in the fact that the whole project was rooted in treating the *Morgan* as an artifact worthy of respect—one that could bring a variety of people together. Layer two can be seen in the museum's commitment to sailing the vessel, thus helping a new generation reanimate a distant past. Layer three is evidenced by the museum's commitment to listening to a diverse range of perspectives and experiences. Finally, the fourth layer is illustrated by the museum's decision to position itself as a forum in which all of the voices could be shared, amplified, and celebrated.

Conclusions

Any good project should raise as many questions as it answers, and the *38th Voyage* certainly has done that. Will it result in a larger and more diverse audience for Mystic Seaport in the long term? What steps will be required for the preservation of a rich archive of digital content? Will the *Morgan* ever sail again? For now, the museum has no official plans to do so. However, if there are compelling reasons to do so in the future (aside from just sailing the vessel), it is possible that a new team and crew will set sail to add other perspectives to the *Morgan*'s story.

The issue of relevance continues to be at the forefront of every museum professional's mind. To remain viable in the twenty-first century, we are tasked with presenting ourselves as not just "nice to have," but essential. The answers to these questions are as diverse and complex as the communities we serve. To help my colleagues, I offer two final thoughts. First, we should not look at collecting and preserving as the approaches of a bygone era in museum administration. Mystic Seaport's need to restore the *Morgan* was the catalyst for everything related to the *38th Voyage*. Preservation can be a catalyst for action. Second, conversations about helping museums and historic sites meet twenty-first-century challenges often involve the phrase "radical change." This idea has plenty of merit, but it can be misunderstood. It does not, by default, entail separating ourselves entirely from the work that earlier generations of museum professionals have done. As we try to plot a course toward the future, museum professionals may also find inspiration by looking back into the work of their predecessors. To help others make use of the past, we would do well to make use of our own.

Notes

1. Joseph Gordon, "The Morgan's Last Stowaway," *The Log of Mystic Seaport* 25, no. 4 (1973): 122–28.

2. Gordon, "The Morgan's Last Stowaway," 124.

3. Susan M. Pearce, "Objects as Meaning; or Narrating the Past," in *Interpreting Objects and Collections* (London: Routledge, 1994), 26.

4. Stephen E. Weil, "From Being about Something to Being for Somebody: The Ongoing Transformation of the American Museum." Harvard University, 325. http://isites.harvard.edu/fs/docs/icb.topic862568.files/Supplementary%20Readings/Weil%201999.pdf.

5. Steven M. Purdy, "Charles W. Morgan Interpretation Handbook." Unpublished manuscript (Mystic Seaport Museum, Mystic, CT, 2014), 66–67.

6. Gail Anderson, ed., *Reinventing the Museum* (Lanham, MD: AltaMira, 2004), 42.

7. Anderson 2004, 39

8. Kelly Boyd, ed., *Encyclopedia of Historians and Historical Writing*. Vol. 2 (London: Fitzroy Dearborn, 1999), 1220.

9. Andrew W. German, "'Seasoned and Weather-Stained,' How the Charles W. Morgan Lives at Age 150," *Sea History* 60 (Winter 1991–1992): 12.

10. Susan S. Funk, Interview by the author. Mystic Seaport Museum, Mystic, CT. January 19, 2016.

11. Edouard A. Stackpole, *The Charles W. Morgan: The Last Wooden Whaleship* (New York: Meredith Press, 1967), 161.

12. Edmund E. Lynch, Memorandum, "Re: CHARLES W. MORGAN and Lift Dock," September 9, 1968 (Mystic, CT: Mystic Seaport Museum), 3.

13. Gainor R. Akin, "The Morgan Floats!" *Windrose*, January 1974, 1.

14. Thomas J. Schlereth, ed., *Material Culture Studies in America* (Lanham, MD: AltaMira, 1999), 164.

15. Schlereth, *Material Culture Studies in America*, 109.

16. Schlereth, *Material Culture Studies in America*, 113.

17. Clarke A. Chambers, "The 'New' Social History, Local History, and Community Empowerment," *Minnesota History* (Spring 1984): 15–16.

18. Chambers, "The 'New' Social History, Local History, and Community Empowerment," 18.

19. Peter Burke, *What Is Cultural History?* (Malden, MA: Polity, 2004), 37.

20. Joshua M. Smith, "Far Beyond Jack Tar: Maritime Historians and the Problem of Audience," *Coriolis* 2, no. 2 (November 2, 2011): 1.

21. Mary K. Bercaw-Edwards, Interview by the author. Mystic Seaport Museum, Mystic, CT. February 4, 2016.

22. German, "'Seasoned and Weather-Stained,'" 12.

23. Nina Simon, *The Participatory Museum* (Santa Cruz, CA: Museums 2.0, 2010), i.

24. Susie Wilkening, *Annual Demographic Update* (Glenmont, NY: REACH Advisors, 2014), 1–8.

25. Elysa Engelman, Interview. Mystic Seaport Museum, Mystic, CT. February 3, 2016.

26. Sam H. Ham, *Interpretation: Making a Difference on Purpose* (Golden, CO: Fulcrum, 2013), 20.

27. Sara Brown, "Last of Her Kind, Whaleship Charles W. Morgan Has Strong Ties to the Vineyard." *Vineyard Gazette*. Last modified July 20, 2014. Accessed February 15, 2016, http://vineyardgazette.com/news/2014/06/20/last-her-kind-whaleship-charles-w-morgan -has-strong-ties-vineyard.

28. George Hein, "The Challenge and Significance of Constructivism." Last modified 2002. Accessed February 15, 2016, http://george-hein.com/papers_online/hoe_2001.html. This website contains the text of a keynote address that was delivered by Hein at the *Hands-On! Europe* conference in London on November 15, 2001. It was originally published in "Proceedings, Hands On! Europe Conference, 2001," London: Discover, 35–42.

29. John Falk and Lynn D. Dierking, *Learning from Museums: Visitor Experience and the Making of Meaning* (Lanham, MD: AltaMira Press, 2000), 12.

30. Ham, *Interpretation*, 152–63.

31. Simon, *The Participatory Museum*, ii.

32. Engelman, Interview, 2016.

CHAPTER 5

LIVING MARITIME HISTORY

The Historic *Belle of Louisville*

Kadie Engstrom

The Beginning

Though we know her today as the *Belle of Louisville*, she was originally named the *Idlewild* when built by James Rees and Sons in 1914 at Pittsburgh, Pennsylvania, for the West Memphis Packet Company. Her owners designed her as a ferry and day packet vessel for moving cargo and carrying passengers. After arriving at her first home port of Memphis, Tennessee, she operated as a ferry between Memphis and West Memphis, Arkansas, while approach roads to a new bridge spanning the Mississippi River were constructed. Freight work and excursion cruises close to home were the primary sources of income.

The Early Years

The *Idlewild* entered service at a time when river cargo handling and travel was beginning to decline, so she enjoyed only a brief career as a day packet, decks laden with produce, bales of cotton, barrels and crates of farm, household, and construction goods, lumber, and sacks of grain—anything that could be moved economically by water, including passengers. She was solid and well-built, with a steel hull that requires little water to float—she draws only five feet of water—and was able to travel on virtually every navigable waterway from the Missouri River to the eastern states.

In the early 1930s, however, as all-weather road surfaces paved the way for a then-infant trucking industry, railroads, and towboats took on more and more freight work. The demand for packet boats decreased dramatically. In search of a new type of business

Figure 5.1 In the spirit of authentic interpretation, the *Belle of Louisville* will occasionally accommodate a shoreside landing, tied off to trees, in the manner of her antebellum predecessors. Photograph by Joel Stone.

trade, the *Idlewild* was converted to service as an excursion boat, and she "tramped" her way along the Ohio, Illinois, Mississippi, and Missouri river systems—stopping at a town along the banks, running short trips for a few days, then moving on up or down the river to another town. To add income for her owners, she often carried cargo picked up in one town and delivered to another.

Sometime during this decade, and to make her more visually appealing for passengers, the *Idlewild's* texas cabin (on the third deck) was lengthened to accommodate more crew members, awnings were added to cover the exterior decks, and Victorian "gingerbread" trim decorated the newly enlarged texas deck roof.

A significant turn of events came in 1930 after Louisville's excursion boat, the *America*, burned beyond use just after Labor Day. Under charter to the Rose Island Company, the *Idlewild* made her first trip to the area in 1931 to spend that summer season running short excursions and trips between Louisville and Rose Island amusement park, about fourteen miles upriver from Louisville. A few independent businessmen had created a thriving entertainment area on a small section of land just above Fourteen Mile Creek on the Indiana shoreline. The *Idlewild* also took people to Fontaine Ferry Park in west Louisville, and fun-loving passengers traveled back and forth between the two amusement parks just as young people today move mercurially from one source of entertainment to another. That charter was the beginning of a long-standing association between the boat and the "Derby City." Though she traveled a vagabond's life for another three years, in 1934 the *Idlewild* returned to Louisville to operate regular excursion trips each season through World War II.

A Brief "Military Career"

During the 1940s when everyone's help was needed to aid the war effort, even though the *Idlewild* continued her excursion trade at Louisville during the summer, when the excursion season ended, she moved further inland for off-season work. She towed oil barges along the Mississippi River—an affectionate misnomer, as barges on the river are pushed, not pulled—and had to be specially rigged for the work, since her sloping and pointed bow was not designed for pushing boats ahead of her. She was fitted out with a set of "tow knees"—two four-foot-tall vertical steel beams attached to either side of the bow—that provided a surface for pressing against the flat ends of the barges and making them easier to propel and control. Besides her towing work, she was used by the United Service Organization (USO) as a floating nightspot for troops stationed at military bases on the Mississippi.

Changing Owners, Changing Names

The boat had several owners during her first three decades; the longest was Henry Meyer, of the St. Louis and Calhoun Packet Company, from 1928 to1947. The *Idlewild* served thirty-three years under her original name, but change was in store when she was sold in 1947 to J. Herod Gorsage. Though the *Idlewild* was destined to remain under that ownership just a short time, in February 1948 she was renamed the *Avalon* to honor the deathbed wish of Ben Winters, who had been Master under Mr. Gorsage. Captain Winters began his long river career aboard a steamer with that name, and he hoped the *Avalon* would be remembered.

She was sold again in the spring of 1948 to a group of investors from Cincinnati, Ohio, and during the next thirteen years the *Avalon* became the most widely traveled river steamer of her size on the country's vast Western river system. It was an exciting life—visiting ports such as Omaha, Nebraska, on the Missouri River; Stillwater, Minnesota, on the St. Croix River; Peoria, Illinois, on the Illinois River; Montgomery, West Virginia, on the Kanawha River; and Nashville, Tennessee, on the Cumberland River.

This stalwart boat was an old hand on the Tennessee River from Knoxville to Chattanooga. She also knew the Mississippi River well between St. Paul, Minnesota, and New Orleans, Louisiana, and the Ohio River between Pittsburgh, Pennsylvania, and Cairo, Illinois. The *Avalon* visited people from all segments of urban and rural society in at least sixteen states and carried the ever-flowing history of our constantly changing nation.

Time for a Facelift

In 1954, diesel replaced coal as the fuel to fire her boilers. A safer, more dependable "telegraph" replaced the original bells-and-gongs communication system between the pilot house and engine room. In the late 1950s, the *Avalon* underwent extensive restoration. The main deck (the first deck just above the hull) and the ballroom deck (the second and open-floored deck) were enclosed to lengthen the boat's operating season. Her smoke stacks were shortened to allow for easier passage under low bridges over shallow rivers, and her pilot house dome was removed and replaced with a flatter roofed structure that offered less wind resistance.

Finding a Home

Though originally scheduled for demolition, in a sadly decrepit state and in need of loving hands, the *Avalon* was sold—for the last time—at auction in Cincinnati in the spring of 1962. With the encouragement and support of former Louisville mayor Charles Farnsley and sitting mayor William Cowger, the highest bid was offered by Jefferson County Judge Executive Marlow Cook, a forward-thinking man with an affection for the boat, a vision for her future as a Louisville landmark, and $34,000 of county funds.

That autumn her name was changed to the *Belle of Louisville*, and under the care and restoration skill of a few dedicated volunteers, the boat began a new life on the south shore of the Ohio River. It took immeasurable hours of constructing, rebuilding, painting, patching, putting up and taking down, testing, wiring, and polishing to make her look and act like a paddlewheel steamer ready for excursion service again. With the perseverance of those who believed in the project and the "never-say-die" scrounging of pieces and parts, she finally found her home and rightful place at the foot of Fourth Street—just in time to turn her bow upriver for her first time-honored and traditional

Figure 5.2   The *Belle of Louisville* approaching her dock near downtown Louisville, Kentucky, on the Ohio River. Photograph by Joel Stone.

Kentucky Derby Festival Great Steamboat Race against the river steamer *Delta Queen* on April 30, 1963.

Today she is recognized as the oldest operating Mississippi River–style steamboat in the world. In 1989 she was named a National Historic Landmark by the US Department of the Interior and is also on the National Register of Historic Places. She is proud to be the legendary lady of a very small and elite group of steam-powered boats still operating on our country's inland rivers.

She turned one hundred years old on October 18, 2014, a feat that has never been equaled by any other American river steamboat; and as the *Belle* steams into the twenty-first century, the vigil for her well-being is constant. Those who have watched her change over the years know without question the place she holds in American history and in the hearts of the people of Louisville, Kentucky.

How She "Fits" in History Today

The *Belle of Louisville* is unique in both river history and in the interpretive museum field. She is the only one of her kind in the United States, still running, that was built during the steamboat era and built as a packet boat. At one time, there were thousands like her traveling on every navigable waterway from the West to East coasts, and from the northern border to the Gulf of Mexico. They were the mainstay for rapid transportation in their time, and the force behind the economic development of the country. Today, there is one remaining representative of that time still operating with the same steam engines that were put on her in 1914—engines, as far as can be known, that were built in the mid-1890s.

Even though she entered the river commerce venture late in the game, so to speak, her construction is very much the construction of the boats of the middle nineteenth century. Designers and builders reached the technological peak of performance by then, and steamboat architecture became somewhat standard in overall features. Though the *Belle* was launched with a steam-assisted "power steering" system, a technology that was new at that time, it was the only major mechanical difference between her and riverboats of the 1850s. Mark Twain, well-known author of classic American literature, was a steamboat cub pilot from 1857 to 1861, and we often say that if he were alive today, he could run this boat.

The steamboat was so common in its day that, in essence, it got lost in history. Many schoolchildren grew up learning from their textbooks that in 1807 Robert Fulton invented the steamboat—often called "Fulton's Folly"—and that it was named the *Clermont*. Neither of those is true, but it has been through relatively recent research and publication that the real understanding of steamboat history has become known to a broader public. In fact, the first steam-powered vessel in this country was launched in August 1787 by John Fitch. Fulton used Fitch's designs and the designs of other inventors of the late eighteenth century to build his own boat twenty years later, the *North River Steamboat*. Fulton never called his boat "Clermont," and never claimed to be the inventor of the steamboat. However, a biography written of him in the early 1800s erroneously stated his contribution to steamboat history, and the story was perpetuated in history books for generations. Unfortunately, for many in the current generation, the steamboat is no longer visible in the American history taught in schools. Without the *Belle of Louisville* as a physical presence, it could easily be lost altogether, with no experiential understanding of the significant part the steamboat played in its time.

Interpreting Her History

People choose to ride the *Belle of Louisville* for a variety of reasons, all offering great opportunities for interpretation. Large groups enjoy a boat that can accommodate as many as eight hundred people. For them, their cruising experience is intended to be a party to a greater or lesser degree. However, especially on public excursions, many people choose to ride because of the historic attributes the boat provides.

Given that the public areas are primarily a set of large, open spaces, history is interpreted differently on each deck. On the main deck (the lowest one), the best interpretation is visual, as passengers can easily see the nineteenth-century technology that runs the boat,

Figure 5.3 The *Belle of Louisville*'s engine room located near the stern, shown here, and the boiler room near the bow, are both visually accessible to passengers. Engineers engage interested guests when unoccupied. Photograph by Joel Stone.

and the engines and steam functions are easy to identify. A long companionway along both sides is a perfect gallery space for large photographs and signage. On the starboard side (right side of the boat facing forward), images show the *Idlewild* under construction and as a packet boat, followed by her evolution over decades through the *Avalon* years and as the *Belle*. Signage at the firebox (boiler room) and in the engine room section describes how things work, and show the "before" and "after" effect of mechanical changes through small photographs. On the port side (left side of the boat facing forward) photographs of other steamboats provide a connection to the era, broadening the understanding of the steamboat as an industry. Engineering crew members add to the onboard interpretation, and are always willing to share their knowledge with interested visitors.

The second deck, commonly known as the boiler deck or the dance floor deck, is used mostly for buffet and concession services. Connections to a sound system allow historians to do narrations from the bandstand area at the stern of that deck that can be heard throughout the boat. A DJ is typically on board to provide entertainment on public cruises; but on cruises when a narration is planned, the bandstand is accessible by all passengers, so they can ask questions and seek clarification. The dance floor deck has been the most altered deck during the boat's century; but while most of historic interpretation does not happen on this deck specifically, one of the boat's most impressive features is the pressed tin ceiling that spans the area between the concession and souvenir stands. It was installed when the boat was built.

The upper, outside decks—the texas and hurricane decks—are meant for viewing the river while underway. Interpretive signs on these decks describe the Captain's Quarters, the only cabin originally built on the boat; the calliope, a thirty-two-key steam-powered organ; and the paddlewheel that propels the boat. Passengers tend to think our calliope is recorded music and that our propulsion is actually provided by propellers—the paddlewheel is just for show. Signage helps dispel those misunderstandings.

For safety reasons, visitors cannot access the roof of the boat where the pilot house (the command center where steering takes place) is located. There is a sign on the texas deck next to the pilot house door that helps people see that steering is done by a human being using the same wheel that was installed on the boat in 1914.

Even with signage and photos, the best interpretation of the boat's history is through narration. A historian more effectively brings out a general history of the boat and describes its impressive features during a cruise, encouraging passengers to explore the boat. People can follow their particular interests, and the historical narration can be customized to the needs of the individuals and groups on board at any given time.

The boat's Education Coordinator has created many printed resources, available to the general public, that cover a wide range of subjects—all describing the steamboat and placing the *Belle* in its historical context. They can be used by teachers to reach classroom needs, or by anyone interested in the steamboat era, the river, or the *Belle* and her sister boats, *Life-Saving Station #10* and the riverboat *Spirit of Jefferson*. The most popular is a brochure that highlights the boat's historic features, and serves as a self-guided tour of the *Belle* that can be used by passengers while they are cruising.

The Challenges

Like most museums and historic sites, the *Belle* depends on the community for her existence. However, because the boat is so unique, the "community" extends to all fifty states and many foreign countries. She is owned by the Louisville Metro government, and receives some financial support as a government agency. Other income comes from ticket sales for cruises, souvenir and concession sales, donations, grants, and foundations. Grants come in the form of financial support, as well as services provided. For example, a local machine company offered to re-bore the *Belle*'s engines at their expense, instead of making a monetary contribution.

Public money, once a plentiful stream, has been greatly reduced over the last ten years. Grants for educational purposes are scarce, but there is some support for unique needs, like re-boring the engines or special programming. A few years ago, the *Belle* creatively pursued a grant for a project that provided photographs and informational signage throughout the boat, illustrating for passengers the boat's operational processes and historical background as they explore during a cruise. The grantors did not define that as an educational need; they saw it as a programming need, and funded it.

Funding, or the lack thereof, is a constant for most historic sites, but dealing with an old, floating vessel has its own challenges. It is particularly difficult—and often impossible—to get pre-made, off-the-shelf mechanical parts for a 102-year-old steamboat. The boat's crew generally has to make or have someone else make replacements for worn out parts, adding to the expense. Maintenance is a constant requirement for any boat, and an expensive undertaking when dealing with several decks, multiple types of equipment, painting, re-decking, replacing worn superstructure, changing windows and frames, building or removing interior features, or taking care of mechanical systems. For the most part, the needs of the boat are managed by the crew or through contracts with local businesses with the right skills to meet the need.

Though sweeping the dance floor can be done by anyone with a broom, many of the skills needed to keep the boat running are specialized, and not found through the general employment market. Most of the engineers, captains, pilots, and mates have come up "through the ranks," and have learned the trade by doing the trade. Because there are only a small number of vessels that are steam-powered, the pool of available, experienced crew members in the United States is very small. This issue will increase in importance as years pass, so teaching our younger crew members the skills they need to take on leadership roles as they grow older is essential.

Captains and pilots must be licensed by an agency of the federal government, and some mates and members of the engineering crew are licensed as well. Achieving a license is an involved process, requiring months—sometimes years—of comprehensive study and on-the-job experience. Those striving for licensing face a very intensive—and costly—testing process, and often must travel long distances to a testing site with no guarantee of success. Occasionally, applicants fail their first attempts and must reapply, thereby extending the process and expense.

Perhaps one of the most significant differences between land-based museums and this steamboat is that operation of the *Belle* is regulated by the US Coast Guard, with

Figure 5.4 The *Belle of Louisville*'s pilot navigates the vessel and communicates with other crew members from the pilot house on the top deck. For safety reasons this area is not open to the public, but is interpreted on the main deck. Image courtesy of the *Belle of Louisville*.

ties to Transportation Authority regulations. Passenger and boat safety is a way of life. The organization must be prepared for unannounced inspections by the Coast Guard or other federal agencies at any time, so the vessel must be boat-shape at all times, with a highly trained crew and monthly data collection. The onboard operational crew is randomly drug-tested, and goes through weekly drills to stay sharp. All personnel are taught and quizzed on safety measures affecting passengers at all levels. Every five years the boat is required to go into dry dock, where she is taken completely out of water for rigorous inspections by the Coast Guard and necessary repairs to make sure she is river-worthy for passenger service.

Because the *Belle* operates an onboard food service, we are regulated by the local county health department and the federal Food and Drug Administration. The county health department does a scheduled inspection prior to the start of the operational season, then both agencies do unannounced inspections as they choose. Again, our food service areas must be ready at all times to be under the watchful eye of health officials.

Meeting the Americans with Disabilities Act requirements has posed challenges, due to the age of the boat and its architectural limitations, but some ingenuity and an understanding of boat construction have helped make access easier for passengers of varying ages and circumstances. Under normal river conditions, our gangway ("stage" on a riverboat) provides an unencumbered entrance and exit between the wharf and the boat; passengers using wheelchairs can roll onto and off the main deck. In addition, both restrooms have a handicapped stall and sink space that allows for wheelchair needs. They are located on the dance floor deck, the second deck, which is accessible for people with mobility issues. In years past, our crew carried an individual in their wheelchair up the forward staircase to the second deck. However, with the installation of a mechanical lift, individuals with non-motorized or motorized wheelchairs can be transported from the main deck to the dance floor without difficulty. There is no access to the upper decks except by staircase, but the second deck offers restrooms, concessions, and heat and air-conditioning.

Beyond the needs of the boat itself, the river poses additional obstacles. While we do not face the problems of low water on the Ohio River, high water can change our cruising schedule with very short notice. One thing for certain: Mother Nature is *always* in charge. If the water overflows the wharf, and is high enough that our landing markers cannot be seen, the boat cannot leave the wharf. Managing disappointed passengers— something that rarely happens with terrestrial structures that can keep their doors open regardless of the weather—is even more challenging when many of them have planned their schedules around the one time they are visiting the Louisville area, and the one day and time they can fit in a steamboat ride.

Unique Cultural Advantages

The *Belle of Louisville* is the only river steamboat in the country to reach the age of one hundred, and is still going strong. Most of the thousands of packet boats built, especially during the nineteenth century, lasted three to five years; so a one-hundred-year-old riverboat is truly a phenomenon. Her builders knew their craft well and built her with a great deal of experience and a steel hull. With care and maintenance along the way—and some luck—the *Belle* has survived to earn the distinction of being the last of her kind.

The boat's one-of-a-kind status gives her an advantage in attracting visitors. People from all over the world are drawn to her and the chance to experience something that can only be experienced at Louisville, Kentucky: a ride on the oldest and most authentic river steamboat in the nation. In some ways, that fact alone is a marketing opportunity at its best. Tourism is a huge industry in Louisville, and the metropolitan area is rich in cultural and historic resources. Louisville is a destination city, and the *Belle* is a highly recognizable icon.

In addition, she is completely unique in the Louisville metropolitan area. There are many sites that tell a portion of Louisville's story as the community grew and changed; there is only one that is still working and doing the same job she was designed for more than a century ago. In an era when people are looking for a way to go back in time to an easier way of life and a reminder of how things used to be, the *Belle* is an attraction at the top of that list. Her audience is broad—she appeals to all ages: youngsters because there are things to see and places to go that cannot be experienced anywhere else in the area; older people because she brings with her a relaxing atmosphere and a slower pace.

To maritime historians and anthropologists, the boat represents a precious living artifact. Journalists and videographers endeavor to capture her many charms.

Charter audiences are varied. Schools choose the *Belle* for field trips because so many elements of her history, mechanics, and architecture align with school curriculum plans, and because written resources are available to help teachers reach their instructional goals. Groups enjoy her because of the vessel's size and versatility. Bus tours are thrilled because we serve a buffet lunch or dinner and provide a unique experience. The public on vacation wants to enjoy the opportunities that are particular to the area. We are encouraged by visitor trends—the public seems increasingly interested in connecting to local history.

At the Heart of the Community

One local historian, said, "The [Ohio River] made Louisville a town, the steamboat made it a city." Originally, everything and everyone depended in some way on the river for their livelihood. While the river is still an essential shipping avenue, as it has been since the first explorers ventured this far into the New World, it is no longer the highway for human transportation as it once was. Now, it is a source of mystique; a short and enjoyable afternoon adventure, with time left in the day to seek out other interesting things to do in the area.

The *Belle of Louisville* sits at Louisville's Fourth Street Wharf, in a location that is familiar for her. When she came to Louisville as the *Idlewild* and the *Avalon*, she landed in a similar location on the waterfront. In the days when commerce depended on the river for moving products and people, businesses vied for close proximity to the city's boat landing. Today, many of those buildings are being used to continue the commerce of the city through cultural or historic sites, or for commercial institutions, like restaurants and nightspots.

The landing's close proximity to the oldest section of downtown Louisville and the easy connection to cultural and historic sites of the community create a perfect avenue for collaborations with related organizations. Many partnerships have proven very successful. Some examples are: a river pirate program with the Frazier History Museum; a presentation for teachers and organizational members of the Sons of the American Revolution; a "river" experience for Girl Scouts and Boy Scouts with the Louisville Water Company and Falls of the Ohio State Park; and field trips for fourth and fifth grade students learning how water is used from the Louisville Water Company, Metropolitan Sewer District, and American Commercial Barge Lines.

Over the years, educational programming has been created for a wide range of groups—for example, a professional theater company, a local college, the genealogy archivist at the public library, and the American Association of State and Local History and United States Life Saving Station Heritage Association conferences. There have been innumerable presentations for community groups, including libraries, historical societies, churches, retirement facilities, schools, and organizations of every type and size. In the Louisville area, the steamboat and the river influenced everyone and everything during the development of the city; today, all the historic sites in the area can be linked together because of their associations with river transportation in some way in the eighteenth, nineteenth, and early twentieth centuries.

From a marketing and facility rental perspective, the *Belle* has the distinct advantage of being able to offer a meal on board, while watching the passing scene. Many passengers enjoy a meal while they cruise, and a catered buffet suits the bill the best. As a large event space, the dance floor—an interior deck two-thirds the length of the boat—is a perfect dining venue. When the buffet service is removed, the dance floor is open. There are also outside decks, so passengers can move from the dance floor to other areas of the boat with ease. Many of our passengers like to explore the nineteenth-century technology that is our engine room, firebox, and steam system. Signage and photographs entice the curious.

In Summary

The historic steamboat *Belle of Louisville* is both an active river vessel offering excursion cruises and the most authentic representative of the steamboat era. In the steamboat's heyday, vessels like the *Belle* were commonplace in every community along navigable rivers, and were the mainstay of the nation's economy. Phil Cole, in *Steamboat Echoes*, says that the building and outfitting of steamboats, and the services necessary to meet the needs of passengers and crew was, at one time, the second largest employer in our country, behind agriculture. When you consider that the entire United States, in the nineteenth century, for example, was 85 percent agriculture and 15 percent town, steamboating was a huge industry. Today, that entire era is represented in one remaining river vessel that builds up a head of steam and takes short cruises, experiencing the river as people did 150 years ago.

The challenges are both physical and economic. The *Belle of Louisville* is an old boat with all the daily accommodations that implies. In return, the fact that she is the last of her kind, and is cared for with sensitivity, respect, and intentional preservation, gives her story even greater importance. It is the story of our nation. Her history is America's history.

CHAPTER 6

PLACE, INDUSTRY, RECREATION

Interpreting a Diverse Maritime Environment

Joel Stone

ONE CHALLENGE that a curatorial team will occasionally encounter is a story so broad and intertwined in the fabric of the community that it is difficult to bring all the pertinent elements to play. Finding appropriate balance drives content and policy decisions in libraries, archives, and collections, but can be especially challenging with the immediacy of museum exhibitions. How do you tell the whole story so that people can easily absorb it and recognize their own story in the overall scheme? And amid the denseness of the narrative, how should various interpretive, interactive, and participatory tools be leveraged to maximize the visitor experience?

This was the situation faced by the staff of the Detroit Historical Society when redesigning the main gallery of the historic Dossin Great Lakes Museum on Belle Isle Park in the Detroit River. The town's waterborne international commerce story is many centuries old, with over three hundred years of history on record. In North America just a handful of cities can claim an older maritime heritage, and Detroit still has very active waterways.

However, diversity and innovation—not longevity—define Detroit's regional maritime legacy. Every manner of maritime commerce and recreation has operated along local shores, and not passively, but in leadership roles and in record-setting numbers.

You're thinking, "Detroit?" Midwestern epicenter of the American auto industry. Multiracial generator of great music. Good theater, sports, and political entertainment (arguably all theater). If you're having trouble redefining Detroit as one of America's major maritime centers, you are not alone. Today, many Detroiters don't know how important ships and boats are to their lives. So the challenge at the Dossin Museum was to fill a modest gallery (130 feet x 30 feet) with as much of the story as possible, making it comprehensible and engaging.

The Back Story

If you're not acquainted with the Great Lakes system, it's worth a look. The watershed contains 85 percent of North America's fresh surface water. Together, the lakes (including the Canadian shore) have more coastline than all the United States saltwater coasts together, not including Alaska. At the beginning of the last century, the Port of Detroit was the busiest waterway in the world. From shipbuilding innovation to watersports mecca, the city's maritime history is broad and deep, from Paleolithic fishing villages to modern container ports.

The full spectrum of commercial and recreational marine activities includes such internationally respected names as Chris-Craft and SeaRay, Detroit and Cleveland Navigation Company, and Bayview Yacht Club—over sixty yacht clubs, in fact, within a short cruise. Prohibition and various wartime activities could be chapters unto themselves. The scope of the business encompasses shipyards, chandlers, steamship lines, resorts, fisheries, government agencies, shipping agents, insurance brokers, admiralty lawyers, architects, engineers, marinas, boatbuilders, boat owners, engine builders, sailmakers, foundries, dry docks, grain elevators, canals, tunnels, rail ferries, passenger ferries, dredges, tugs, fireboats, survey vessels, lightships, yachts, charter vessels, tour boats, racing boats, recreational diving, paddleboards and kayaks, maritime unions, unique nomenclature, and America's only waterborne post office, the *J. W. Westcott II*, zip code 48222.

Detroit doesn't have tides, salt spray, or sponge harvesting, but by any other measure Detroit is an international port city. Historian Catherine Cangany, in her 2014 book *Frontier Seaport*, argues that the town has been an Atlantic entrepôt with ties to Russia and China prior to the American Revolution. This remains true, and the city and museum are dedicated to fostering an understanding of that heritage.[1]

The Dossin Museum is the repository that holds that story. First housed in the retired schooner *J. T. Wing* in 1949, the collection is an amalgam of commercial, recreational, and governmental material—archival and artifactual—gathered at a time when many maritime industries were ceasing operations in the area. Detroit's boat racing Dossin family and the City of Detroit funded a new museum that opened in 1960, the first facility built specifically to interpret Great Lakes history. The collection has since grown to include tens of thousands of maritime-related objects and ephemera.

The Project

Between 2008 and 2013, the Society successfully managed a $21 million campaign to renovate two museums for which they had assumed managerial control from the City of Detroit in 2006. The Dossin Museum project was phase two of the *Past>Forward* comprehensive initiative, undertaken during the worst days of the Great Recession. With tremendous support from the citizens of the city, the campaign was a success.

Figure 6.1 As the last working sailing ship on the Great Lakes, the schooner *J. T. Wing* became the *Museum of the Great Lakes* in 1949. It was permanently dry-docked adjacent to Belle Isle Park in Detroit, Michigan. Image courtesy of the Detroit Historical Society Collection.

The process employed to renovate the Dossin Great Lakes Museum was honed during the renovation, several months earlier, of seven galleries at the Detroit Historical Museum. The process itself involved first gathering input from constituent groups and stakeholders, refining their feedback into major themes and subthemes, then creating thematic content maps that helped define interpretive direction and gallery layout.

The museum's main gallery was ready for a major makeover. During the first fifty years, various installations had carved the 3,900-square foot space into noncohesive segments. In addition, efforts to "tell the whole story" had packed the room with artifacts

Figure 6.2 Initially, the Dossin Great Lakes Museum had a single large gallery which featured a fine model collection and various topical displays. Image courtesy of the Detroit Historical Society Collection.

and interpretation, limiting the room available for group tours and events. Decades of dwindling budgets while under municipal management left little funding for new display cases, plinths, or vitrine bases; many were original to the museum. There were six interactive features available; two were long out of order, and one involved letting visitors sit on an artifact.

The intention of the *Past>Forward* campaign's physical plant renewal was to bring the museums up to current best-practice standards whenever possible. The city used Federal Recovery Act funds to update the Dossin's HVAC system with new boilers and air-conditioning units. Renovation plans included: updated security; all new lighting, including LED fixtures throughout; and a new all-museum public address system. The main gallery was gutted to its cinder block walls and steel plate ceiling, allowing a *tabula rasa* for designers.

Working with the consulting firm Good Design Group, an advisory committee was formed to define the exhibition's audience and identify elements deemed most important to that audience. The committee was made up of select curatorial and interpretive staff members (vice president to docents), trustees, scholars, maritime professionals, and educators.

Meetings convened at the museum by Good Design Group worked through a process of idea generation and prioritization. Following introductions and a walkthrough of the existing space, the first gathering plunged into Big Picture thoughts, starting with

"What stories can we tell better than anyone else?" and "What do visitors need to know when they leave?" Content brainstorming revealed some primary themes, and prompted further questions: How do we define the audience for this facility? How can we create synergy with the Detroit Historical Museum, through exhibits, publicity, programs, fundraising, and volunteers? Who is our competition for similar experiences, what do they offer, and how can we complement it?

Answering the first question was critical, and after some discussion our audience was defined by two constituencies: casual visitors, and mariners and marine aficionados.

The casual crowd included both traditional and new groups: grandparents with grandkids, families, school groups, tourists to Belle Isle, and facility renters. The first three have been served by the Dossin for many years. Indeed, the intergenerational conversation between adults and children has always been a strong component of the museum's approach and strength; most adult visitors have some affinity to maritime history, and most docents have a maritime background. School tours, long a part of the museum's educational programming, is supported by an excellent docent corps.

Hampered by the gallery's crowded physical layout, the redesign had to address the group experience. Casual tourism was a newly revised industry in Detroit at this time, and that segment was accounted for. On the horizon was the incorporation of Belle Isle Park into the Michigan State Park system, and the potential for vastly expanded group tour opportunities. Finally, the museum was increasingly popular for events, generating significant income as well as casual visitors who would otherwise never come through the door; catering requirements were a consideration in the gallery redesign.

The second constituency was defined as serious maritime "folks." Museum consultant Barry Lord referred to them as the "community of origin"—they or their ancestors were involved with, or created context for, the history being presented.[2] Longtime supporters of the museum including the Great Lakes Maritime Institute, Marine Historical Society of Detroit, International Shipmasters' Association, Historic Memorials Committee, many local yacht clubs, and hundreds of former mariners. It also included numerous affinity groups who promoted and preserved lighthouses, steam whistles, outboard motors, ship models, photographs, and memorabilia from industries as varied as shipbuilding and hydroplane racing.

There was a natural crossover between the two constituencies. The first audience might be considered our prime target for entertaining and educating, the second our primary support segment—and our best critic. For both, the finished gallery had to be exciting and approachable, and continue the tradition of integrity that the museum and the Detroit Historical Society represent.

Addressing the other questions stated earlier: How can we create synergy with the Detroit Historical Museum (DHM, which the society also manages), through exhibits, publicity, programs, fundraising, and volunteers? The DHM includes elements of the maritime story in its exhibits, particularly related to the industrial, cultural, Underground Railroad, and Arsenal of Democracy aspects. Cross-promotion was a natural opportunity and proved successful, raising the profile of the Dossin Museum to a broad metropolitan audience. Its location—on an island park that an ever-smaller-segment of suburban residents visited—had left it isolated. Inclusion in the society's public relations material helped, offering a much higher profile than before. Making it the focus of society publicity and programming focusing on marine topics breathed new life into the society's development efforts; due to the city's long involvement with the water, it was not surprising that many funders and supporters had a maritime affinity.

Who is our competition for similar experiences, what do they offer, and how can we complement it? This turned out to be an important and timely consideration. While there was little competition when the museum opened in 1960, fifty years later the Great Lakes boasted more than a dozen major maritime museums or sites, another dozen regional maritime museums, two dozen museum ships, and almost fifty lighthouse museums. At the time of the Dossin redesign in 2012, a Lake Erie organization (Historical Society of the Great Lakes) was moving to a new exhibition facility in Toledo, Ohio—about an eighty-minute drive south—that included a marina and a classic Great Lakes freighter museum ship. While the Dossin Museum had been unique on Lakes in 1961, the plethora of ship-related offerings suggested a reevaluation of the building's focus.

In addition, the Detroit area had seen a growth in museum-based organizations. Besides the venerable destination lately rebranded as The Henry Ford and the iconic Detroit Institute of Arts, the last five decades had seen the birth of a major African American history facility, a significant science center, and numerous community historic villages, agricultural campuses, and military sites.

Considering this altered cultural landscape, the stakeholders revisited the institution's purpose. The museum's name and decades-long mission dictated that the central theme remain the entire Great Lakes system. As a major thoroughfare on that system, Detroit and the Lakes were wedded long ago. However, the exhibit committee decided that a new curatorial focus should favor stories of the Detroit River region, extending from the foot of Lake Huron to the north, to the Michigan border on Lake Erie, south of the city. It was time for the Dossin Great Lakes Museum to tell Detroit area stories.

When Good Design Group convened stakeholders for a second meeting, key questions emerged, including: Did we get the overall content correct? Was there anything forgotten, or anything that doesn't fit? What are the key messages or "takeaways" that visitors need to understand? How should the information be organized? What techniques are appropriate?

Lively discussion eventually narrowed the focus to a manageable list of essential exhibit topics and presentation ideals. Good Design Group then translated the results into Content Maps with conceptual silos and universal themes.

The two content maps featured four conceptual buckets—*Place*, *Industry*, *Recreation*, and International *Border*. It became clear that some type of *Timeline* element was needed, to help put the *Place*, *Industry*, and *Recreation* in perspective. The *Border* concept stood alone and was eventually merged beautifully into the *Timeline* grouping.

Horizontally across all silos, universal themes emerged—boats, water, and people. Maritime history *is* boats. Similarly important is water; without it there are no boats. Without people there are no boatbuilders, sailors, passengers, agents, shippers, consumers, fishermen, or divers.

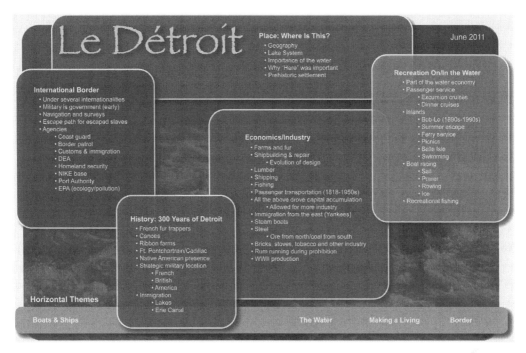

Figure 6.3 The Content Map developed by Good Design Group defined necessary elements to be included in the "Built by the River" exhibition, and helped discern interpretive emphasis and organization. Image courtesy of the Detroit Historical Society Collection.

Notably, an important aspect of the maritime world was consciously omitted from the exhibition—the *Natural Sciences*, including limnology, bathometry, zoology, and ecology. The reasons were simple. First, the island park where the museum operates is also home to a botanical conservatory, an aquarium, and a nature zoo which each tell various portions of this story. Second, it was decided that these topics could be better addressed in temporary installations. For example, in 2014 the exhibits team opened "Troubled Waters" about regional water ecology, the display beautifully enhanced by historic bird and fish mounts, some a century old, loaned by the Cranbrook Institute of Science in nearby Bloomfield Hills.

Floor plans emerged naturally out of the Content Maps. It was clear that contextually *Place* was a great introduction to the gallery. Two succeeding bays addressed the *Industry* and *Recreation* aspects of the Detroit maritime, reflecting the largest silos. *Timeline* and *Border* elements were dedicated to a long contiguous wall space running the length of the gallery.

One of the needs of the new design included large, flexible spaces within the gallery to allow school groups and event caterers plenty of elbow room. At the same time, there needed to be a sense of intimacy, to encourage engagement with the content, as well as a general direction for people to follow—a cogency. In part this intimacy was created with colors: ceiling and upper wall colors unified the room. Various areas were distinguished by harmonized hues, textures and wall treatments—three-dimensional river murals, factory exterior, steamship bulkhead—accented by artifacts, images, and text. Visual flow in the gallery was created through the artistic use of carpet tiles cut to represent the river that flows through all aspects of Detroit's history.

In preparing to address the stories told in five major areas, curatorial and collections staff compiled a list of potential assets within the society's holdings that would complement some of the proposed props and hands-on elements identified during planning meetings. Because of the presence the Dossin Museum has enjoyed in the region, the collection is significant, and the opportunities myriad. A couple of examples can serve to illustrate: the first supporters of the museum were model shipbuilders, and as a result the museum has an extensive collection of superb models built to the same one-eighth scale—a wonderful interpretive tool when comparing an early French trading ship with today's massive freighters. Additionally, the archives hold tens of thousands of photographs and published ephemera related to all aspects of the Great Lakes maritime.

Place

When developing the first section, two significant items were included to define *Place*—a three-dimensional map of the region, and a classic old wooded ship's wheel and its brass pedestal. The map has been a feature in the building since its opening, illustrating the lakes in great detail, both in breadth and depth. It was refurbished, and installed in a fresh enclosure. Button-activated mini-lights on the map's face were reconfigured to indicate major ports and their cargoes—significant to the notion of *Place*, as Detroit's positional bulb lit with nearly every push.

One highlight of the previous gallery was a place where a person could stand at a ship's wheel and pretend to steer. This concept was included in the new design as one of the first things guests see upon entering the gallery. Behind the wheel is a backlit silhouette of the Detroit River, and interpretation that identifies the birth and growth of the many communities along the shore. Interpretation in this section includes an immersive lesson about Detroit's place in the early North American fur trade. A very sturdy replica canoe juts from the wall, and allows visitors the opportunity to put on a buckskin jacket, review some local correspondence between fur traders, then sit in the boat and "paddle" away. Both the ship's wheel and canoe are popular photo opportunities.

One final addition was made to this section when an interested sponsor stepped forward. The museum maintains a popular "River Cam" on the roof that is accessible and operable from any computer in the world. Unfortunately, despite its popularity, the webcam was not accessible in the museum. On the surface, it seemed unnecessary; visitors could simply walk to the SS *William Clay Ford* pilot house installation and have the same experience—live. However, the pilot house is not accessible to some mobility impaired guests, and the website's additional information (weather, approaching ships, etc.) was potentially helpful to all guests. With the support of a local corporation and uber-volunteer Neil Schultheiss, who maintains the camera year-round (it is mounted on a mast forty feet above the river), a kiosk now offers the web experience as you enter the gallery.

Figure 6.4 To interpret the idea of *Place* in the "Built by the River" exhibition, the intro-ductory section features a three-dimensional map of the Great Lakes, as well as space to interpret Detroit's involvement in the North American fur trade. Image courtesy of the Detroit Historical Society Collection.

Timeline and Border

Continuing along the right side of the gallery, past the step-in canoe, two convex-faced cases were constructed and placed at equal intervals along the length of the wall. The first case included the installation of Native American artifacts, models showing the growth of ships through the eighteenth and mid-nineteenth century, a section of old Fort Detroit stockade post—coincidently converted to a desk set and used by President Eisenhower to sign the St. Lawrence Seaway Act—and images of the waterfront. The second case picks up the story and takes it into the mid-twentieth century, including shipbuilding, surveying, navigation, and security. Again, ship models demonstrate growth, and artifacts represent technological developments.

Between the two cases, a large mural of an early map of the Detroit River reinforces the theme of *Place*. Five didactic panels discuss the river's significance in prehistory, the colonial era, during the War of 1812 and the American Civil War, as an active terminus on the Underground Railroad, and its role in nationwide alcohol distribution during Prohibition. Two pedestals with vitrines and artifacts accompany the text, as well as some in-gallery seating.

Industry

When developing the next two sections, *Industry* and *Recreation*, the exhibits team recog-nized the inherent overlap—commercial shipyards make pleasure yachts and speedboats, and fishermen prefer mass-produced outboard motors, rods, and lures. To delineate the two main themes, the curatorial team asked, "What will our visitors easily understand? How will they expect to see this material presented?" In the end the division was simple:

Figure 6.5 Casework in the "Built by the River" exhibition allowed topical stories to be accompanied by artifacts. Toward the end of the gallery, part of the *Recreation* story is told. Image courtesy of the Detroit Historical Society Collection.

work versus play. *Industry* was the business-related facets of the maritime that include manufacturing, technology, innovation, communication, advertising, and service industries. *Recreation* suggests fun in so many ways: watching boats, paddling boats, sailing boats, racing boats, riding on boats, building boats, and living on boats.[3]

The *Industry* installation—the business side of maritime—panned around the middle C-shaped bay of the mid-gallery. Three subthemes were identified: shipbuilding and engine building; professional skills, including ship handling, cargoes, employment, and communication; and passenger traffic—ferries, excursion boats, and cruise ships.

Below large format images and text panels representing the subthemes, a "wharf" treatment—built at kid-friendly height—was designed as the platform for several interactive complements to the various themes.

Recreation

The *Recreation* section makes a natural transition from the leisure pastime of riding river steamboats, as an *Industry*, to the more active and entertaining topics of sailing, fishing, rowing, canoeing, boat racing, and amusement parks. Physically, this space is a mirror of the initial *Place* section; a roughly square footprint with a transverse traffic pattern that leads to an open portal into further galleries. It was decided that one area would represent active boating—small boats and racing—and the other represent passive boating—parks, resorts, and excursion destinations.

Figure 6.6 The *Industry* portion of the "Built by the River" exhibition features several interactive elements, including boatbuilding and knot tying. Image courtesy of the Detroit Historical Society Collection.

Set prominently into the space, on the active side, is a "speedboat"—one that anyone can drive. Facing the bow, looking through the windshield, visitors can choose to drive a hydroplane jockeying for starting position at the start of a Gold Cup Race on the Detroit River, heading to the start of the Port Huron to Mackinac sailboat race, and cruising in an Anchor Bay iceboat at sixty miles per hour. The boat is fully accessible and allows guest seating in the stern; the transom section provides perfect context and a perfect traffic barrier.

I mentioned that flow was important to the development of the footprint. You will see from the floor plan illustration that when entering "Built by the River," the *Place* section has all attractions set outside of the main traffic flow, running transversely through the space. People are pulled to the side if they wish to linger, and guests intent on galleries further into the museum pass freely. The carpet colors intentionally suggest this flow. The *Industry* section is intentionally a backwater—a place where lingering and discovery are encouraged and conversational groups can gather outside of the main traffic area. *Recreation*, again with a transverse flow, offered a challenge. The footprint of most boats is relatively the same; pointy on the front, flat on the back. The bow (pointy end) of our imaginary "speedboat" snuggled well into one corner of the space, with the stern tailing out—into the middle of the room. Potentially, this was a big traffic flow issue. Instead,

Figure 6.7 The "Built by the River" exhibition concludes by examining waterborne recreation, including sports like racing and fishing, as well as pastimes like lakeside amusement parks and resorts. Image courtesy of the Detroit Historical Society Collection.

the bow and stern became separate units, with teak-and-maple flooring, but no sides, creating the appropriate visual footprint. The stern unit (about five-feet wide, thirty-inches tall, and a four-foot depth that included a bench facing the video monitor at the bow) serves as an effective traffic diversion. Depending on the type of guests or events in progress, traffic can actively flow in five different directions.

Returning to the historical aspect of the *Recreation* exhibit, racing transitions to active relaxation like canoeing, yachting, boating, fishing—and the companies based in the area that catered to that trade. The active relaxation theme transitions, across the room, to the more passive aspects of marine-based recreation. This includes daily ferry trips for commuters and exciting ventures to local amusement parks, when the boat trip was as memorable as the destination. For millions, simply watching boats steaming past a picnic blanket along the shore was entertainment. Public parks, resorts, and river towns hold the story of several generations reveling in the reliable and picturesque vistas offered by the area's rivers, lakes, and the largest freshwater delta in the world.

Throughout both the "active" and "passive" side of the gallery, artifacts, videos, and memory-captures allow generations of people in southern Michigan and Ontario to understand and interact with Detroit's recreational past. From this area guests are free to double back and revisit favorite areas in the gallery, or move on to other exhibitions in the museum.

Conclusion

By all accounts the "Built by the River" installation has been a resounding success. Its nine "active" and six "passive" interactive elements blend well with the static, more traditional didactics and casework. Artifacts—the keystone of a good exhibit—are prominently displayed, including sixteen ship and engine models, a cornerstone of the collection. At any given time, over thirty models are on display throughout the museum. The overall design of the room—colors, scenery, images, text, wall treatments, carpet—flows cleanly and invitingly.

Attendance skyrocketed between 2013 and 2016, although not entirely attributable to the new exhibition. The society's two museums were reopened using a family-friendly Free Admission model that has proved popular and successful. Additionally, when the island joined the Michigan State Park system, visitorship to the island and its attractions greatly increased. Together, these factors conspired to put attendance at the Dossin Great Lakes Museum, over the past decade, on a very encouraging trajectory.

Each interpretive situation is unique, but there are common forms and techniques that can be leveraged to simplify the task of defining exhibition focus and understanding optimal balance. At the Dossin Great Lakes Museum, the process included stakeholder input, content maps, and creative space design. The committee process assured that many diverse topics and voices were considered, assuring balance. Content maps defined how a wide array of subjects could be logically distributed in the gallery using the themes of *Place*, *Industry*, and *Recreation*. Creative space design addressed traffic flow and venue-use concerns, while allowing for the liberal inclusion of artifacts, interactives, and a variety of information delivery opportunities.

Notes

1. Catherine Cangany, *Frontier Seaport* (Chicago: University of Chicago, 2014), 1–7.
2. Barry Lord, *The Manual of Museum Learning* (Lanham, MD: AltaMira, 2015), 15.
3. It should be noted that Great Lakes folks call everything from a canoe to a one-thousand-foot freighter a "boat." Please forgive the occasional colloquialism—JLS.

CHAPTER 7

UNDERWATER ARCHAEOLOGICAL PRESERVES, PARKS, AND TRAILS

A Florida Perspective

Franklin H. Price

O N JANUARY 4, 1866, the steam tug USS *Narcissus*, along with her consort USS *Althea*, ran into heavy weather off Egmont Key, Florida. USS *Narcissus* had served with the West Gulf Blockading Squadron during the Civil War, and took part in the Battle of Mobile Bay, where Admiral Farragut had uttered the words "Damn the torpedoes," and ordered his command to follow him into the battle. Soon afterward, the tug struck one of the mines while paying out the anchor and was sunk, but then raised and repaired. Taking different routes into Tampa, USS *Narcissus* ran aground on a sand bar within sight of USS *Althea*. While trying to free herself, USS *Narcissus'* steam boiler exploded, and all on board were lost.[1] Today the site is memorialized as one of Florida's Underwater Archaeological Preserves, part of a program that combines public access and historic interpretation to foster feelings of value and stewardship toward maritime heritage and nautical archaeology.

Heritage managers in Florida are faced with a tricky problem. How can they make shipwrecks accessible and protect them at the same time for the public benefit? Protection depends upon a variety of factors. One of the most important is public appreciation, which requires interpretation and engaging the public as shareholders. Heritage managers in the United States and abroad employ a variety of management strategies, but differ on the subject of site accessibility. Florida's example offers a solution to the dilemma, balancing access with preservation by involving the public, whose participation is the cornerstone of the program.[2] This chapter will describe one strategy that the Florida

Figure 7.1 This photograph of the officers of the USS *Narcissus* was taken in Pensacola, Florida, about a month before the vessel's boiler exploded during a storm, killing all on board. It was found by a couple from Alberta, Canada, hidden behind a framed Victorian-era drawing. Photograph signed by J. M. Young. Image from the State Archives of Florida, courtesy of Al and Nina Page.

Department of State uses to address these challenges, by creating Underwater Archaeological Preserves that are accessible to both the diving and nondiving public.[3] The example of the most recent Preserve, USS *Narcissus*, will illustrate the unique public-oriented process that Florida implements to dedicate its Preserves.

Before addressing this topic directly, the legal framework of state and federal laws that protects historic shipwrecks in Florida's sovereign submerged bottomlands should be explored.[4] Two of the numerous laws that especially affect Florida archaeologists are the federal Abandoned Shipwreck Act and the Florida Historical Resources Act. At the federal level, the management of abandoned historic vessels passed from federal to state hands with the Abandoned Shipwreck Act of 1988. This law supersedes Admiralty law, or law of finds. It also contains provisions for free access to shipwreck sites, where appropriate, easing concerns within the sport diving community that this legislation would signal an end to legal wreck exploration. Under the law states make their own decisions regarding the disposition of historic shipwrecks in their waters. The most important piece of Florida legislation regarding its submerged heritage is the Florida Historical Resources Act of 1967, which states that "all treasure trove, artifacts, and such objects having intrinsic or historical and archaeological value which have been abandoned on state-owned lands or state-owned sovereignty submerged lands shall belong to the state with the title thereto vested in the Division of Historical Resources of the Department of State for the purposes of administration and protection."[5] Artifacts may not be removed from a historic site on submerged lands without authorization. Permits are provided under rule 1A-31, which allows for commercial salvage, and 1A-32, which regulates academic and public archaeological projects. The Florida Historical Resources Act stresses that the resources belong to the people of Florida, a distinction that is at the essence of Florida's Underwater Archaeological Preserves program. Historical resources are to be shared, not to be put off-limits to the public, not to be removed from the seafloor and sold for the profit of individuals or companies, but to be conserved not only for the people of today, but for those of the future.

Approaches to Submerged
Archaeological Preserves and Parks

The legal framework, combined with a mandate to both preserve the past and make it publicly accessible, can present heritage managers with a dilemma of choosing between access and preservation. Either a site can be off-limits, perhaps giving it a higher likelihood of being preserved, or it can be open to visitation, potentially leaving it vulnerable to looting or vandalism. These are two apparently dichotomous choices for managing sites, but they do not have to be. In response, submerged heritage management strategies have run the gamut between closed and open sites. Some sites are off-limits to visitors, others are restricted to chaperoned access, while some have unsupervised and limited access, and still others have unsupervised and unfettered access. Next is a brief look at selected sites in the United States and around the world that exemplify differing management tactics.

Some shipwrecks, because of their significance, fragility, sensitivity to damage, or other factors, are best left undisturbed. A prime example of a restricted site is USS *Arizona*, which is both a historic site of international significance and a war grave. The interior is off-limits, even to divers from the US National Park Service.[6]

A chaperoned approach provides heritage managers with the ability to control both the diver's experience and the amount of interaction with the shipwreck. This not only allays fears of site damage, but also allows heritage managers to capitalize on the site visit as a means to educate the public on issues of archaeology, history, heritage, and conservation. For example, divers need licenses to dive certain protected sites in the United Kingdom, where matters are further complicated by murky legalities surrounding ownership.[7] These same sites, however, are featured as trails such as at *Coronation*, *Hazardous*, Norman's Bay, and HMS *Colossus*, the latter of which has seen 1,100 divers since 2009.[8] Near Naples, Italy, the submerged Roman ruins at Baia are interpreted for divers, where local dive operators offer government approved tours to the public.[9] On some UK wrecks covered under the Protected Wrecks Act, English Heritage works together with what they term Affiliated Volunteers to survey a site.[10] A chaperoned approach has been employed by heritage managers themselves, as at *Queen Anne's Revenge* in North Carolina and *Célèbre* in Nova Scotia,[11] or by approved diving operations such as at the wreck of a B-29 bomber in Nevada and Portugal's Tróia I site.[12] The Italian government's *Sopritendenza del Mare* has underwater heritage trails at several locations, expanding in recent years.[13] At Pantilleria Island, for example, divers may access the site only through sanctioned diving centers that also serve as stewards of the resource, maintaining the trails.[14]

Another approach is to allow unchaperoned access, but to require diver registration, both as a means to quantify visitation and to deter vandalism and looting. If authorities are aware when a particular diver is visiting a site, it is argued, this would dissuade would-be vandals or looters from damaging or destroying submerged resources. This idea, with various permutations, has been employed in Maryland on the *U-1105*, in New York at Lake George, and in Australia on SS *Duckenfield*.[15] Other examples of this strategy can be found in Vermont, where divers are required to seasonally register to visit preserves, and in North Carolina, which has a voluntary registration with its SS *Huron* preserve.[16] This choice has mixed results regarding the preservation of sites, but is mostly effective.

Florida is far from alone in its choice of open access. Numerous other agencies also choose an unrestricted management strategy for shipwreck sites. The wide variety of examples includes an anchor field in the Azores, Caesaria Maritima in Israel, California's Underwater Parks, the *Kronprinz Gustav* Dive Park in Finland, Marine Protected Areas in the Dominican Republic, and U-Boats off the US Atlantic seaboard, among many others.[17]

Other governments are easing their access to submerged archaeological sites. A notable example is Greece, where scuba diving has been highly restricted. A recent opening of the waters to divers has led to a concomitant rise in the level of engagement between the diving community and maritime archaeologists, potentially resulting in the establishment of future underwater archaeological parks.[18] This unique situation will allow for an assessment of what happens with underwater heritage before and after it is opened to the public. It will be interesting to learn if the result is greater or lesser preservation of archaeological sites, as well as to note changes in public attitudes toward submerged heritage.

Education through Access

Unfettered access to archaeological sites can appear to be at odds with the goals of preservation, and in some instances this is the case.[19] However, inclusion and access to a shipwreck site can provide an education that gives the public a sense of ownership that places intrinsic value on the site. The shipwreck becomes what it actually is by statute— *theirs*.[20] With this sense of shared ownership comes increased value and a feeling that communities are stewards, which leads to more conservation, not less. Florida's Preserves program suggests that with the proper education the public will protect and preserve shipwrecks.[21] Much like the change that has occurred in the dive community during the past several decades regarding the protection of coral reefs, a similar shift is occurring regarding shipwreck sites. Divers are realizing that they are stewards of the deep, not only of the natural world, but of our shared cultural legacy as well. This is where Florida's Underwater Archaeological Preserves program stands, with the argument that education through access helps the cause of historic preservation. And even beyond that, the Preserves program uses public involvement as a key component of the program, so that local communities buy-in to ideals of preservation and conservation. This entire process centers on education. Heritage managers are responsible for interpreting a site properly to show waterfront communities the value of the archaeology in their area.[22] As Roger Smith has written, "In this way, shipwrecks come to be adopted by local citizens as a unique part of their neighborhood."[23]

Development of Florida's Preserves Program

Florida's first Underwater Archaeological Preserve, *Urca de Lima*, was dedicated in 1987, but the idea for the program goes back much earlier. In fact, the St. Lucie County Board of Commissioners petitioned Senator Robert Williams in 1968 for a shipwreck to be set aside from commercial salvage so that there would be something left of the 1715 fleet for future generations to see.[24] Even earlier, a similarly unheeded appeal came from the Florida Keys, where in 1964 civic groups, including the Florida Keys Underwater Guides Association, the Florida Upper Keys Chamber of Commerce, and the Monroe County Advertising Commission wrote to the governor of Florida to ask that wrecks from the 1733 plate fleet be protected.[25] These requests were ahead of their time, and no action was taken.

In the 1980s the St. Lucie County Historical Commission again asked the state to protect one of the 1715 plate fleet wrecks, this time a shipwreck that had been salvaged, *Urca de Lima*. Dedication of this Preserve, along with the second Preserve, *San Pedro*, laid the groundwork and provided a template for future Preserves.[26]

Public participation is a key aspect that makes Florida's Underwater Archaeological preserves different from other parks, trails, and preserves. Each of the Preserves dedicated since *Urca de Lima* has, by design, included the public in the process, from the nomination onward.

Florida now has twelve Underwater Archaeological Preserves, situated around the state. Moving west to east, they are: USS *Massachusetts*, the nation's oldest battleship hull and veteran of the Spanish-American War; SS *Tarpon*, a freighter lost in a storm in 1937; *Vamar*, a tramp freighter that once carried airplanes for Admiral Byrd's flight over the south pole; *City of Hawkinsville*, the largest steamboat to ply the Suwannee River; USS *Narcissus*, a US Navy steam tug lost outside Tampa Bay; *Regina*, a molasses barge sunk off Bradenton Beach; *San Pedro*, a galleon of the 1733 fleet, in shallow water near Islamorada; *Half Moon*, a German-built racing yacht now off Key Biscayne; SS *Copenhagen*, a freighter on the Pompano Ledge off Lauderdale-by-the-Sea; *Lofthus*, a bark near Boynton Beach that once painted fake gun ports on her hull to deter pirates; *Georges Valentine*, another bark lost in a terrible storm near the House of Refuge at Gilbert Bar; and *Urca de Lima*, a store ship of the 1715 plate fleet, lost off Ft. Pierce.

Figure 7.2 The iron-hulled lumber vessel *Georges Valentine* was swept ashore near Gilbert's Bar (shoal) on Henderson Island, Florida. Efforts of a keeper at the nearby House of Refuge, seen in the background, saved seven of the twelve men on board. A plaque is installed near the House of Refuge Museum at Gilbert's Bar. Photograph courtesy of the Historical Society of Martin County.

The dedication of USS *Narcissus*, Florida's most recent Underwater Archaeological Preserve, serves to illustrate the Preserves' process, one that, as heritage managers have rightly argued, involves the public for the benefit of preservation.[27] Florida's Underwater Archaeological Preserves follow a series of steps beginning with nomination and progressing through dedication and interpretation. While not codified, these steps have been followed with each dedication. In the case of the latest Preserve, USS *Narcissus* was nominated by the Florida Aquarium in Tampa, and South Eastern Archaeological Services.[28] The site had already been archaeologically investigated, usually the second step in the process to evaluate its candidacy for Preserve status. The Division of Historical Resources in Tallahassee considered the nomination in light of several criteria, including that the sites are located in state waters, have safe public access, both "recognizable features" and "abundant marine life," and they must be sites with verifiable identities.[29] USS *Narcissus* met these criteria: the shipwreck had been studied and identified, was accessible, near the coast of Egmont Key in shallow water, and had an array of marine life including baitfish, gray snapper, sheepshead, stone crab, southern stingrays, even seahorses and Goliath grouper.

Dive shops, local government, clubs, area businesses, and others were contacted to measure interest in the site becoming a Preserve. Meetings were held locally, and the importance of community involvement and stewardship was stressed. A "Friends of the Preserve" group was created in coordination with the Florida Aquarium and with assistance from the Florida Public Archaeology Network. A site survey had already been completed, allowing state archaeologists to move on to the next step, the creation of a formal proposal sent to dive businesses, local government, individuals, and other interested parties. Its dissemination was accompanied by a press release furnished to the media.[30] With USS *Narcissus*, the proposal was also sent to the US Navy History and Heritage Command, because unique among the Preserves, the shipwreck itself remains property of the US Navy under the Sunken Military Craft Act of 2005.

USS *Narcissus* received strong public, governmental, and organizational support, so the state considered the proposal accepted. This paved the way for the opening ceremony and the placement of a plaque and underwater monument on site. These were deployed with the assistance of the US Coast Guard, as well as the nominators, South Eastern Archaeological Services and the Florida Aquarium. The Aquarium graciously hosted the dedication ceremony in January 2015, which included speeches by various dignitaries, while a live video feed unveiled the monument on the seafloor. The tenth step, to nominate the site to the National Register of Historic Places, followed soon after and the state also created an array of interpretive products.

Interpretation

Since the success of Florida's program hinges on education, the state provides a wide variety of media for interpreting and enjoying the sites. Materials include onsite components, print handouts, and online text, and visual media, site plans, photographs, and video. While the archaeological and historical significance of each site is stressed, the ecological and biological aspect of a shipwreck is also featured. Interpretation of sites is designed to reach a wide swath of the general public, from divers and snorkelers to history buffs, students to educators to anyone interested in maritime heritage. The goal is increased awareness of Florida's shared maritime heritage so that people know that they may visit and appreciate Florida's submerged cultural resources.

Most of the sites have a bronze plaque bolted and cemented into a concrete monument underwater adjacent to the shipwreck that identifies the site and briefly explains its history and significance. The plaque's location, at the shipwreck itself, lends gravity, imparting to the visitor a tangible sense of historical and archaeological importance. The monuments are usually trapezoidal in shape for stability on the seafloor; however, this is not always the case. At the recently dedicated USS *Narcissus* Preserve, the Friends group chose to install the bronze plaque into a reef ball, an ovoid-shaped concrete construction complete with holes that provide a home for corals, sponges, and reef fish. A structure that would become a sea life habitat was fitting because the Florida Aquarium in Tampa was integral to the Preserve's nomination and ultimate dedication.

The few plaques that have not been deployed are on land at locations accessible to the public. An example of this is the plaque for *Georges Valentine*, lost near Stuart. The plaque is installed near the House of Refuge Museum at Gilbert's Bar, on Hutchinson Island. Visitors can see an exhibit on the shipwreck at the museum, and read the bronze plaque officially designating it as an Underwater Archaeological Preserve, all while looking out over the same waters where the bark wrecked more than a century ago.

Figure 7.3 The Florida Underwater Preserves Council placed an underwater plaque near the anchor of the British cargo ship *Copenhagen*, which hit a reef at full speed in 1900 while filled with Pennsylvania coal. Photograph courtesy of Howie Grapek/www .grapek.com.

In print, each Preserve is interpreted in a trifold brochure provided by the Florida Department of State. Brochures feature the history, the location, a site description, and the shipwreck's role as an Underwater Archaeological Preserve. A painting of the vessel underway graces the front cover, as well as the Florida Department of State's logo, and mention of partners who made the Preserve possible. Each brochure contains underwater photographs, a location map, coordinates in latitude and longitude, and a site plan. Thousands of brochures are delivered annually to dive shops around the state. Additionally, all twelve wrecks appear on a poster promoting the Preserves program and website.

In order to enhance the diving and snorkeling experience, an underwater guide is also available. These laminated guides orient visitors on the site and assist in interpreting what is being seen and experienced underwater. Each two-sided sheet features the history and location of the site and has a site plan for reference on the seafloor. Stressing a conservation ethic, visitors are made aware of heritage laws and urged to "Take only photos and leave only bubbles!"

Florida's Underwater Archaeological Preserves belong to all of the people of Florida, not only divers and snorkelers. With this in mind, the Florida Department of State created the website, Museums in the Sea (museumsinthesea.com), that allows the general public to experience these sites without leaving home.[31] Each of the twelve shipwrecks has its own series of pages, as well as links to the brochure and underwater guide, and

Figure 7.4 Image of the Shipwreck Poster offered by the Florida Department of State to promote the Florida Shipwreck Preserves and MuseumsInTheSea.com. Image courtesy of the Florida Department of State.

narrated videos. The videos, titled "Take an Underwater Tour," "Learn about the History," and "Discover the Biology," take the viewer into three aspects of each Preserve: the site itself, its history, and the sea life that now calls each shipwreck home. The video tour identifies site components, giving a diver or snorkeler a sense of what to expect, but also shows the nondiving public or armchair enthusiast what it is like to experience these shipwrecks firsthand. The next video briefs the visitor on the history of each site, its importance and significance, as well as the lore, stories, and details of the human tragedy surrounding each wreck. The last video in the series gives the viewer an appreciation of an often-overlooked aspect of shipwrecks, that they become artificial reefs, often home to thriving biological communities. Accomplishing this through an introduction to some of the local species, these videos convey the biological importance of the sites.

In sum, the array of interpretive materials allows everyone, diver and nondiver alike, to experience Florida's submerged heritage. This idea is central to the Preserves program and in accordance with both Florida law and federal legislation like the Abandoned Shipwreck Act. These sites are shared resources belonging to the people of Florida. Proper interpretation allows the sites to fulfill the mandate, defined in state law, that created them in the first place. They are important, as is the need to learn what we can from our maritime history and share that knowledge as widely as possible.

Challenges, Impacts, and Results

Managing Florida's Underwater Archaeological Preserves is not without its challenges. A significant one is geography. The physical distances involved within the state of Florida can be quite large. State archaeologists can only visit so many sites per year, and are responsible not only for the Preserves program, but for the archaeology of all of Florida's sovereign submerged lands.

Another challenge is that the sites are underwater. Heritage managers often fight a "finders keepers" mentality regarding submerged cultural heritage.[32] This is where the experiment of public involvement and education comes into play. Policing these sites is logistically impossible, so the local community is called upon as stewards of the resource.[33] Thus far, this has worked to keep the sites free from vandalism and looting. Aside from minor incidents on *San Pedro*, the Preserves have been left alone for future generations of divers to visit and enjoy.[34]

A third challenge has been keeping momentum with Friends groups at some Preserves. Since they often center around a few strong personalities, sometimes these groups slowly dissolve with the absence of a specific leader, or as the old guard falls away. Local communities are encouraged to take the lead. For some Preserves this requires more direct involvement from the state. In the case of USS *Narcissus*, partnership with the Florida Public Archaeology Network will be beneficial, providing a local institutional partner. In other instances, local involvement has been remarkable. At the SS *Copenhagen* Preserve, for example, the Town of Lauderdale-by-the-Sea has celebrated the Preserve with a commissioned illustration, two interpretive plaques, a T-shirt, a laminated guide, and have decorated one of their utility structures with an SS *Copenhagen* theme, among other efforts.

Promotion has had a significant impact on the program. Total visitation to the Preserves by divers and snorkelers has hovered close to thirty thousand annually in 2013 and 2014. The large amount of exposure generated by the web page has exceeded expectations; website visits grew from 625,000 to more than 1,000,000 in the same time span.[35]

Designation of Preserve status imbues an air of official importance and lends a sense of place that affects how a community views their shipwreck. National Register status has a similarly positive effect. All of the Preserves except USS *Narcissus* are listed on the National Register of Historic Places, and USS *Narcissus* is in the nomination process. National Register status gives the sites added legitimacy, becoming a point of local pride and a selling point for visitation.

Preserves have a substantial economic impact on area diving businesses. Dive shops near SS *Copenhagen*, as an example, derive large portions of their income from taking visitors to the Preserve. At *Vamar* another dive shop profits from the Preserve, bringing hundreds of people to the site each year, accounting for a substantial part of their overall business as a dive operator. *Vamar* and SS *Copenhagen* are visited often because they share the common factors of shallow depth, proximity to dive operators, marine life, rich history, and remaining structure. They serve to illustrate how a community economically benefits from taking a stake in its heritage. As Scott-Ireton has written, "Businesses support preserves, because they draw tourist dollars and additional visitors."[36] The realization that shipwreck conservation makes sound economic sense is nothing new. In fact, the economic value of *in situ* shipwrecks was not lost on the pioneer proponents of ship-wreck preservation in Florida. As the Monroe County Advertising Commission wrote to Florida's governor in 1964, "the underwater beauty of a wreck housing hundreds of fish or a mound of cannon balls is directly beneficial to our economy while concerted salvage operations would destroy permanently the lure of these wrecks."[37]

Conclusion

With the dedication of USS *Narcissus* in 2015, Florida now has twelve Underwater Archaeological Preserves. *Narcissus* joins the other eleven as examples of maritime public archaeology, and part of an experiment in heritage management that brings waterfront communities into the equation. Although one of numerous submerged heritage preserve, park, and trail programs worldwide, Florida is unique in its methodological inclusion of the public in every step of the creation process. Some might see it as a gamble that public involvement and education will lead to greater site protection and preservation, but in the case of Florida's Underwater Archaeological Preserves, public engagement has been the key ingredient to a successful management strategy.

Notes

1. W. F. Kilgore, "Letter to Commander US Steamer *Sagamore*," January 8, 1866. Record Group 45, HG—Groundings, Strandings, Founderings, and Sinkings. Box No. 179. US Steamer *Althea* (Washington, D.C.: Office of Naval Records and Library); "Naval Intelligence: Changes in the Various Squadrons—Movement of the Vessels," *New York Times*, January 22, 1866, 2; "The United States Steamer *Narcissus*: Further Details from Ensign Lannan," *New York Times*, February 4, 1866, 8; "Shipwrecks: Loss of the United States Steamer *Narcissus*, with all on Board," *New York Herald*, February 4, 1866, 1; "Navy Bulletin," *New York Herald*, February 6, 1866, 8; David Dixon Porter, *The Naval History of the Civil War* (New York: Sherman Publishing Company, 1886), 573; Paul H. Silverstone, *Warships of the Civil War Navies* (Annapolis, MD: Naval Institute Press, 1989); Melissa N. T. Morris, "USS *Narcissus*: The Role of the Tugboat in the American Civil War" (M.A. thesis, University of West Florida, 2011).

2. Della Scott-Ireton, "Florida's Underwater Archaeological Preserves," in *Submerged Cultural Resource Management: Preserving and Interpreting our Sunken Maritime Heritage*, eds. James D. Spirek and Della Scott-Ireton (New York: Kluwer Academic/Plenum Press, 2003), 101.

3. For previous synopses of the Preserves program see Roger C. Smith, "Florida's Underwater Archaeological Preserves," in *Underwater Archaeology Proceedings from the Society for Historical Archaeology Conference 1991*, ed. John D. Broadwater (Germantown, MD: Society for Historical Archaeology, 1991), 43–46; Scott-Ireton, "Florida's Underwater Archaeological Preserves," 95–105; Franklin H. Price, "Florida's Underwater Archaeological Preserves: Public Participation as an Approach to Submerged Heritage Management," *Public Archaeology* 12(4) (2013): 221–41; Franklin H. Price, "Florida's Underwater Archaeological Preserves 2013 Visitation and Conditions Assessment" (Tallahassee: Florida Bureau of Archaeological Research, 2014); Franklin H. Price, "Florida's Underwater Archaeological Preserves 2014 Visitation and Conditions Assessment" (Tallahassee: Florida Bureau of Archaeological Research, 2015).

4. Pertinent federal legislation also includes the Antiquities Act of 1906, the Historic Preservation Act of 1966, the Archaeological Resources Protection Act of 1979, and the Sunken Military Craft Act of 2005, among others.

5. Chapter 267.061, Florida Historical Resources Act.

6. David L. Conlin and Matthew A. Russell, "Site Formation Processes Once Removed: Pushing the Boundaries of Interdisciplinary Maritime Archaeology," in *ACUA Underwater Archaeology Proceedings 2009*, eds. E. Laanela and J. Moore (Germantown, MD: Advisory Council on Underwater Archaeology, 2009), 83–90.

7. English Heritage, "Advisory Committee of Historic Wreck Sites Annual Report 2009" (London: Department for Culture, Media and Sport, 2010) [accessed January 25, 2016]. Available at http://www.english-heritage.org.uk/publications/achws-annual-report-2009/achws-2009-10-ann-rep.pdf; Ian Oxley, "Who Owns England's Marine Historic Assets and Why Does It Matter? English Heritage's Work towards Understanding the Opportunities and Threats, and the Development of Solutions and Constructive Engagement with Owners," in *ACUA Underwater Archaeology Proceedings 2014*, eds. Charles Dagneau and Karolyn Gauvin (Germantown, MD: Advisory Council on Underwater Archaeology, 2014), 229–33.

8. Alison James, "Researching, Protecting and Managing England's Marine Historic Environment," in *ACUA Underwater Archaeology Proceedings 2013*, eds. Charles Dagneau and Karolyn Gauvin (Germantown, MD: Advisory Council on Underwater Archaeology, 2013), 177.

9. Michele Stefanile, "Research, Protection, and Musealization in an Underwater Archaeological Park: The Case of Baia (Naples, Italy)," in *Actas de las IV Jornadas de Jovens em Investigação Arqueológica* (Faro: Promontoria Monográfica, 2012), 57–63.

10. James, "Researching, Protecting and Managing England's Marine Historic Environment," 175.

11. Daniel La Roche, "A Review of Cultural Resource Management Experiences in Presenting Canada's Submerged Heritage," in *Submerged Cultural Resource Management: Preserving and Interpreting Our Sunken Maritime Heritage*, eds. James D. Spirek and Della Scott-Ireton (New York: Kluwer Academic/Plenum Press, 2003), 19–41; Mark Wilde-Ramsing and Lauren Hermley, "Diver Awareness Program: QAR Dive Down," in *Out of the Blue: Public Interpretation of Maritime Cultural Resources*, eds. John H. Jameson and Della Scott-Ireton (New York: Springer, 2007), 127–44.

12. David L. Conlin and Larry E. Murphy, Lake Meade National Recreation Area B-29 Management Plan: Technical Report No. 23 (Santa Fe: National Park Service Submerged Resources Center, 2006); Alexandre Monteiro, Underwater Archaeological Trails and Preserves in Portugal (Lisbon: Instituto de Arqueologia e Paleociências, Faculdade de Ciências Sociais e Humanas, Universidade Nova de Lisboa, 2013).

13. Sebastiano Tusa, "Research, Protection and Evaluation of Sicilian and Mediterranean Cultural Heritage," *Conservation Science in Cultural Heritage* 2009(9): 79–112.

14. Leonardo Albelli, Massimiliano Secci, and Pier Giorgio I. Spanu, "The Roman Conquest of Pantilleria through Recent Underwater Investigations: From Discovery to Public Outreach and Public Access to Maritime Cultural Heritage," in *ACUA Underwater Archaeology Proceedings 2014*, eds. Charles Dagneau and Karolyn Gauvin (Germantown, MD: Advisory Council on Underwater Archaeology, 2014), 345–55.

15. D. M. Nutley, "Ten Years of Shipwreck Access and Management Practices," in *Maritime Archaeology in Australia: A Reader*, eds. M. Staniforth and M. Hyde (Blackwood, Australia: Southern Archaeology, 2001), 277–81; Susan B. M. Langley, "Historic Shipwreck Preserves in Maryland," in *Submerged Cultural Resource Management: Preserving and Interpreting Our Sunken Maritime Heritage*, eds. James D. Spirek and Della Scott-Ireton (New York: Kluwer Academic/Plenum Press, 2003), 45–55; Joseph W. Zarzynski, "Lake George, New York: Making Shipwrecks Speak," in *Out of the Blue: Public Interpretation of Maritime Cultural Resources*, eds. John H. Jameson and Della Scott-Ireton (New York: Springer, 2007), 19–32; Joseph W. Zarzynski, David

J. Decker, Peter J. Pepe, and Steven C. Resler, "Painting the Water Blue: The New York State Underwater Blueway Trail," in *ACUA Underwater Archaeology Proceedings 2007*, ed. Victor Mastone (Germantown, MD: Advisory Council on Underwater Archaeology, 2007), 151–56.

16. Joe D. Friday Jr., "The History, Archaeology, and Current Status of the Wreck of the USS *Huron*," in *Underwater Archaeology Proceedings from the Society for Historical Archaeology Conference*, ed. John D. Broadwater (Germantown, MD: Society for Historical Archaeology, 1991), 51–53; Arthur B. Cohn, "Lake Champlain's Underwater Archaeological Preserve Program: Reasonable Access to Appropriate Sites," in *Submerged Cultural Resource Management: Preserving and Interpreting Our Sunken Maritime Heritage*, eds. James D. Spirek and Della Scott-Ireton (New York: Kluwer Academic/Plenum Press, 2003), 88; Richard Lawrence, "From National Tragedy to Cultural Treasure: The USS *Huron* Historic Shipwreck Preserve," in *Submerged Cultural Resource Management: Preserving and Interpreting Our Sunken Maritime Heritage*, eds. James D. Spirek and Della Scott-Ireton (New York: Kluwer Academic/Plenum Press, 2003), 69.

17. Sheli O. Smith, "Frolic *Archaeological Survey*" (Columbus, OH: PAST Foundation, 2005); Sarah Arenson, "The Underwater Archaeological Park at Herod's Sunken Harbor of Sebastos (Caesaria Maritima)," *Leon Recanati Institute for Maritime Studies News* 32(2006): 14–16; Frederick H. Hanselmann and Charles D. Beeker, "Establishing Marine Protected Areas in the Dominican Republic: A Model for Sustainable Preservation," in *ACUA Underwater Archaeology Proceedings 2008*, eds. Susan Langley and Victor Mastone (Germantown, MD: Advisory Council on Underwater Archaeology, 2008), 52–61; Charles D. Beeker and Frederick H. Hanselmann, "The Wreck of the *Cara Merchant*: Investigations of Captain Kidd's Lost Ship," in *ACUA Underwater Archaeology Proceedings 2009*, eds. E. Laanela and J. Moore (Germantown, MD: Advisory Council on Underwater Archaeology, 2009), 219–26; Sallamaria Tikkanen, "Case Studies of Existing Underwater Trails," in *Nordic Blue Parks: Nordic Perspectives on Underwater Natural and Cultural Heritage*, eds. K. O'Brien, S. Tikkannen, C. Lindblad, P. Flyg, A. Olsson, O. Uldum, I. Aarestad, and D. Naevdal (Copenhagen: Nordic Council of Ministers, 2011), 19–32; Christelle Chouzenoux, *Caractérisation et Typologie du Cimitière des Ancres* [Characterization and Typology of the Anchor Graveyard] (M.A. thesis, Universidade Fernando Pessoa, Portugal, 2011).

18. Panagotis Georgopoulos and Tatiana Fragkopoulou, "Underwater Archaeological Parks in Greece: The Cases of Methoni Bay—Sapienza Island and Northern Sporades, from a Culture of Prohibition to a Culture of Engagement," in *ACUA Underwater Archaeology Proceedings 2013*, eds. Colin Breen and Wes Forsythe (Germantown, MD: Advisory Council on Underwater Archaeology, 2013), 191–96.

19. Todd Hannahs, "Underwater Parks vs. Preserves: Data or Access," in *Submerged Cultural Resource Management: Preserving and Interpreting Our Sunken Maritime Heritage*, eds. James D. Spirek and Della A. Scott-Ireton (New York: Kluwer Academic/Plenum Press, 2003), 14.

20. Roger C. Smith, "Florida's Underwater Archaeological Preserves," 45.

21. Roger C. Smith, "Florida's Underwater Archaeological Preserves," 43–46; Scott-Ireton, "Florida's Underwater Archaeological Preserves," 95–105; Della A. Scott-Ireton, "The Value of Public Education and Interpretation in Submerged Cultural Resource Management," in *Out of the Blue: Public Interpretation of Maritime Cultural Resources*, eds. James H. Jameson Jr. and Della A. Scott-Ireton (New York: Springer, 2007), 19–32; Jennifer F. McKinnon and Toni L. Carrell, eds., *The Underwater Archaeology of a Pacific Battlefield: The Battle of Saipan* (New York: Springer, 2015).

22. Della Scott-Ireton, "Preserves, Parks, and Trails: Strategy and Response in Submerged Cultural Resource Management" (PhD diss., Florida State University, 2005).

23. Smith, "Florida's Underwater Archaeological Preserves," 45.

24. St. Lucie County Board of Commissioners, Letter to Senator Robert Williams, April 24, 1968, Florida Master Site File, Tallahassee.

25. Roger C. Smith, "Foreword," in *Submerged Cultural Resource Management: Preserving and Interpreting Our Sunken Maritime Heritage*, eds. James D. Spirek and Della A. Scott-Ireton (New York: Kluwer Academic/Plenum Press, 2003), vii–viii.

26. Smith, "Florida's Underwater Archaeological Preserves," 43–46.

27. Smith, "Florida's Underwater Archaeological Preserves," 43–46; Scott-Ireton, "Florida's Underwater Archaeological Preserves," 95–105; Scott-Ireton, "The Value of Public Education and Interpretation in Submerged Cultural Resource Management," 19–32.

28. Florida Bureau of Archaeological Research, "A Proposal to Establish the Shipwreck USS *Narcissus* as a State Underwater Archaeological Preserve" (Tallahassee: Florida Bureau of Archaeological Research, 2011).

29. Scott-Ireton, "Florida's Underwater Archaeological Preserves," 97.

30. Florida Bureau of Archaeological Research, "A Proposal to Establish the Shipwreck USS *Narcissus* as a State Underwater Archaeological Preserve."

31. museumsinthesea.com

32. Della Scott-Ireton, "Preserves, Parks, and Trails: Strategy and Response in Submerged Cultural Resource Management" (PhD diss., Florida State University, 2005), 2, 4.

33. Smith, "Florida's Underwater Archaeological Preserves," 43–46; Scott-Ireton, "Preserves, Parks, and Trails: Strategy and Response in Submerged Cultural Resource Management."

34. Roger C. Smith, "Memorandum re: *San Pedro* Wreck Site and Park Update," November 7, 1988 (Tallahassee: Bureau of Archaeological Research, 1988); Pat Wells, "Crisis and Miscellaneous Incident Report No. A38386: *San Pedro* Underwater Archaeological Preserve" (Florida Department of Natural Resources, 1995).

35. Price, "Florida's Underwater Archaeological Preserves 2013 Visitation and Conditions Assessment"; Price, "Florida's Underwater Archaeological Preserves 2014 Visitation and Conditions Assessment."

36. Scott-Ireton, "Florida's Underwater Archaeological Preserves," 101.

37. Smith, "Foreword," vii.

CHAPTER 8

MARITIME ARCHAEOLOGY AS "EVIDENCE-BASED STORYTELLING"

Daniel Harrison

> There is a quiet horror about the Great Lakes which grows as one revisits them. Fresh water has no right or call to dip over the horizon, pulling down and pushing up hulls of big steamers, no right to tread the slow, deep sea dance-step between wrinkled cliffs; nor to roar in on weed and sand beaches between vast headlands that run out for leagues into bays and sea fog. Lake Superior is all the same stuff towns pay taxes for (fresh water), but it engulfs and wrecks and drives ashore like a fully accredited ocean—a hideous thing to find in the heart of a continent.
>
> —RUDYARD KIPLING

WHEN MARITIME interpreters encounter historical situations so new and fresh that the facts and context are sketchy, or entirely nonexistent, it requires that they delve into primary interpretation, endeavoring to decipher the story so that it can be told.

The two cases presented in this chapter offer a glimpse into such situations. One examines an assemblage of artifacts from a single site dating from British colonial rule in the latter part of the eighteenth century. The other case analyzes multiple sites within a complex and dynamic maritime landscape over the course of the nineteenth and early twentieth centuries.

Both cases are situated in the waters near Detroit, Michigan—a problematic context for the interpreter, who must address the popular supposition that the region has little

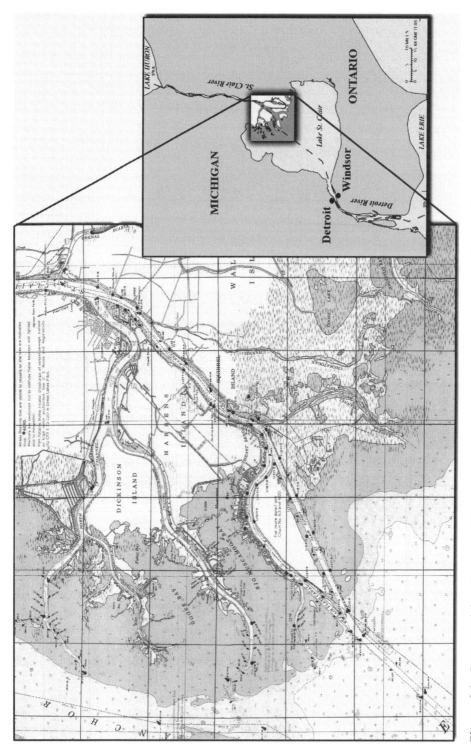

Figure 8.1 Between lakes Huron and Erie are many important submerged assets. The St. Clair River "Flats," represented by the chart, and the downtown Detroit riverfront are locations ripe for multidisciplinary interpretation. Image by Joel Stone.

history of interest prior to industrialization and urbanization, and that these recent processes have eradicated whatever archaeological record might have existed. By turning to the submerged cultural landscape, the maritime archaeologist recovers not only artifacts, but the oft-neglected narrative of shoreside communities. Faced with the task of reinventing itself in the postindustrial era, urban centers like Detroit can best begin to rediscover their past underwater.

The choice of the Great Lakes for a discussion of maritime archaeology may at first seem suspect, but no less an authority than Kipling, who had seen the world, notes that the Great Lakes qualify as "a fully accredited ocean."[1] From an archaeological perspective, most material culture, particularly metal and organic, preserves better submerged than on dry land, and better in freshwater than seawater.[2] This has resulted in an archaeological record that spans the postglacial epoch to the very present. The inundation of nine-thousand-year-old sites by rising lake levels has preserved interpretable evidence, lithic and organic, of Paleo-Indian culture,[3] and the epic "gales of November" have sent thousands of vessels to the bottom, where they are still being found to this day, beautifully preserved.

It is a commonplace observation that an underwater deposition event results in the creation of a "time capsule."[4] The first case study arguably fits this description. My second case, however, demonstrates that the careers of shipwrecks can continue in our lives, individually and collectively. Considered thus, submerged cultural resources may be seen, in the parlance of the *annaliste* historians, both in terms of événement and *la longue durée*—that is, specific historic events and long-term underlying socioeconomic structures, which are uniquely evidenced in their material culture.[5] Moreover, the very act of

Figure 8.2 This British four-pound cannon barrel feels the sun again after more than two hundred years on the bottom of the Detroit River, a stone's throw from the city's main convention center. Photograph courtesy of Joel Stone.

opening a time capsule, even after two centuries or more, places it once more in relation to the present—and the future.

Case Study 1: The "Case of the Corroded Cannon"

On October 5, 2011, a rusted iron cannon barrel, covered with invasive zebra mussels, broke the surface of the Detroit River. Discovered by the Detroit Police Department's Underwater Recovery Team, it was transferred to the Detroit Historical Society and placed in an improvised wet storage tank, where it remained for nearly a year. I was engaged to undertake its conservation and interpretation as a doctoral student at Wayne State University. With invaluable assistance from the Cranbrook Institute of Science in Bloomfield Hills, the gun was immersed in an acrylic tank and, showcased in a public exhibit about the Great Lakes, started the slow process of electrolysis. As the surface of the cannon gradually emerged, the exhibit presented an unfolding mystery ("The Case of the Corroded Cannon"). An exciting element of public involvement occurred when we periodically removed the barrel from its tank and invited visiting schoolchildren to clean the gun's surface with toothbrushes, carefully exposing the diagnostic markings that would help us determine its identity and history. While the conservation process was ongoing, I undertook a three-pronged investigation aimed at explaining not only the identity of the gun on the reef, but the larger historical context that led to its deposition.

Beginning in 1984, five similar cannons, all "four-pounders" (so termed for the weight of the iron shot they fired), had been recovered from the same submerged feature: a sandbar known locally as "Chicken Bone Reef," just offshore from the heart of the old waterfront, near the site of Fort Pontchartrain. Prior to recovering the latest gun, dubbed Cannon 6 or C6, police divers recorded its position using GPS, side-scan sonar, and photographs of the gun *in situ*. The previous five finds were not so well documented, but three guns recovered in 1987 were found disposed in a triangle approximately thirty meters on each side. This effectively ruled out their having been spilled from a capsizing barge, as had been conjectured—one would expect a much more compact pattern. My initial sleuthing answered only the question of *Where*, as I turned to the archives with my remaining questions.

Primary sources documented the gradual escalation of ordnance deployed at Detroit by its defenders and its attackers. Essentially, it represented a "frontier Arms Race" between French, British, and American forces, ending only after 1815. This aspect of historical research, once nearly as challenging (and as dusty and dirty) as archaeology itself, has been rendered far more manageable by three developments: archival digitization projects; online journal databases with powerful search engines; and collaborative library networks.

I looked to archival evidence for the answers to three questions about the "biographies" of the six artifacts in my assemblage: first, how did they come to Detroit; second, what was their career there; and third, how did they come to be in the Detroit River? The answers lay in the historical context of the Great Lakes during the colonial period. Fortunately, British administrators were prolific correspondents and makers of inventories.

Figure 8.3 A view of Detroit, July 25, 1794. Signed E. H., likely Lieutenant Edmund Henn. At the end of British occupation in 1796, Detroit was almost a century old and the largest Great Lakes settlement west of New York. Image courtesy of the Burton Historical Collection, Detroit Public Library.

By treating artillery pieces as an index of British strategic priorities and tracing their movements, I was able to reconstruct the milieu in which the Detroit River guns existed.

While the position of Detroit, like that of Michilimackinac, was highly strategic, the function of both outposts was more economic than military. Contemporary descriptions of the ordnance at Fort Pontchartrain changed little between French and British colonial rule: a handful of smaller cannons, small-bore swivel guns, and a mortar or two. With the American Revolution, the British at Detroit were exposed to the threat of attack—not by water, which they controlled, but by land. Commanders begged for spare ordnance, and Detroit quickly became a veritable magnet for aged iron cannons of all sizes, as shown by successive inventories of its armaments. The deterrent strategy worked, and threatened American attacks never materialized.

In the decade following the Revolutionary War, Detroit's Fort Lernoult stood heavily armed as the British, determined to retain control of their trade routes through the upper Great Lakes, fortified their key positions on American soil in violation of the 1783 Treaty of Paris. As the new Americans pushed into the Ohio country, it became clear that the British strategic position was becoming untenable. Following Anthony Wayne's victory at Fallen Timbers in August of 1794, orders were given to vacate the posts at Michilimackinac, Fort Miami (near present-day Toledo, Ohio), and Detroit. In a directive dated

January 25, 1796, Sir Guy Carleton, Governor-in-Chief of the Canadas, ordered John Graves Simcoe, Lieutenant-General of Upper Canada, to "cause General Surveys to be held without delay on all the King's Stores and effects, and make returns of all such as shall be found unfit for use, not worth removing or impracticable to remove, that *orders may be given for their destruction, or otherwise*, as the case may require" (emphasis added).[6] Considering the January date of the order, I conjectured that the four-pounders were deliberately discarded in compliance with Carleton's order, and that this was accomplished by sliding them onto the frozen river. The spacing observed in the trio of guns recovered in 1987 is consistent with placing them at safe distances from each other on the ice.[7]

Thus, the archival search produced evidence of how the iron four-pounders came to be at Fort Detroit, how they accumulated there, and, when combined with the evidence from their deposition, the circumstances under which they were discarded. What these two lines of inquiry could not answer was why these particular guns were "not worth removing." For that, only the artifacts themselves could provide the answer.

The fact that a total of six cannons, all of the same caliber, had been recovered in close association indicated that C6 was one artifact in an assemblage. Each gun was documented in a database (dimensions, condition, and markings), including two *comparanda*: a four-pounder which had been recovered in the shallows of Lake Erie near Monroe in the early nineteenth century, and a four-pounder located at Fort Malden, Ontario, at the mouth of the Detroit River. These became C7 and C8, respectively.

Besides their common caliber, the Detroit River assemblage showed considerable consistency in one respect: they were all old. One outlier was dated to pre-1715; the rest clustered in the late 1740s. The newest would have been nearly a half-century old when the decision was made in 1796 to discard it. A greater degree of variation was observed in their provenance. Four were cast under military contract, of which only one bore the Royal Ordnance Board proofing mark; the rest had markings indicating they had passed lesser quality standards, including two that were marked as having been acquired and resold by a used armaments dealer in London. One had been made for the commercial market, while the sixth was French. The greatest, and most significant, variability was the degree of bore damage; five of the six were well worn. The guns had likely incurred their wear in the Continental wars of the mid-1700s or the French and Indian War (1754–1763). They were no longer fit for frontline duty, but they weren't all unserviceable.

The presence of at least one serviceable discarded gun featuring a high grade of proofing and minimal bore wear indicated that four-pounders, regardless of their condition, were considered expendable by the retreating British: "not worth removing," yet not to be allowed to fall into the hands of the American upstarts. It is significant that the British made the extra effort to place the guns on the reef, actually sliding the guns past deeper water close to the shore. The reef can be seen in Figure 8.3, indicated by the exposed ribs of a hulk in the lower-right corner, and just offshore from the nearest road from the fort.

Case Closed? "The Case of the Corroded Cannon" led, step by step, from the *événement* of its discard in the winter of 1796, to its explication of the *longue durée*—a "frontier arms race" waged on the Great Lakes from the arrival of Cadillac in 1701 to the

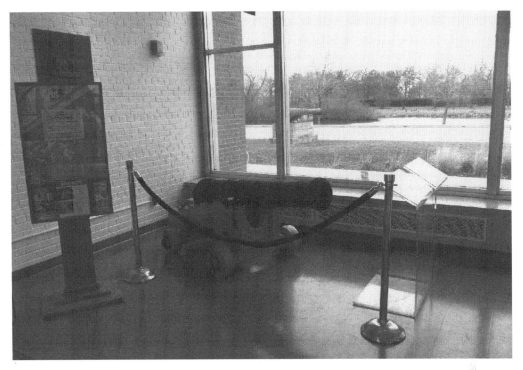

Figure 8.4 Following conservation, the recovered cannon was installed on a reproduction carriage in the foyer of the Dossin Great Lakes Museum in Detroit. Media coverage of the recovery reached around the world, featuring the police divers who found and donated the object. Photograph courtesy of the Detroit Historical Society.

War of 1812. Based on the knowable circumstances and the archaeological record, this offers what I feel is the best fit for defining the circumstances and motivation behind this specific depositional event.

While the eighteen-month conservation process was underway, preparations were made to install cannon C6 at the Dossin Great Lakes Museum on Detroit's Belle Isle Park. Members of the Society's Collections and Interpretation department developed plans for presentation, interpretation, and public interaction.

Based on the advice of armament experts, an artisan was contracted to replicate a wooden naval carriage—most likely in frontier Detroit. It was decided to feature the installation in the Dossin's glass-plated, north-facing vestibule, with the advantage of allowing visitors to see the cannon after museum hours. Because of its obvious durability, sunlight wasn't going to damage the barrel and—an added bonus—we could allow people to touch it. The piece is stanchioned off for safety reasons (temptingly climbable and pinch points), but the muzzle is within reach. Two informational panels trace both the gun's eighteenth-century and twenty-first-century histories. The unveiling event was attended by members of the dive team that recovered the tube, as well as DPD senior staff; each received a small vial of iron that was removed during the conservation process. Both the recovery and the unveiling events garnered international media attention. Five of the eight barrels are on public display at various locations, and are revisiting their interpretive signage to reflect our present state of knowledge.

What is critical to point out in conclusion is that the interpretation of this cannon rests in equal measure upon textual (official communiqués, inventories), contextual (the spatial relationships between fort, reef, and guns), and artifactual evidence (the properties of the guns themselves). Not only is the whole greater than the sum of its parts, it is unachievable in the absence of any element. This robust relationship is the hallmark of historical archaeology; maritime archaeology offers the added benefit of frequently preserving *in situ* not only the artifacts, but the interpretable spatial relationships between and among the features of the landscape, even when that landscape has been as drastically altered as the urbanized Detroit waterfront.

Case Study 2: "A Very Intricate, Tortuous, and Difficult Channel"—The St. Clair Flats

Similarly resting its analysis on the interdependency of text, context, and material culture, the next case scales the analysis up a level, both spatially and temporally. The "frontier arms race" study analyzed a single depositional event (the discard of guns) at a single site (Chicken Bone Reef), in a way that articulated with the larger sweep of historical events and contemporary military practice. In this case, we will look at multiple depositional events (ships sinkings), resulting in the formation of multiple sites (shipwrecks) across a large, complex, and dynamic landscape, over a century of dramatic historical events and evolving maritime practice.

In chronological terms, the two cases flow one into the other, as the urbanization that began to transform the waterfront of eighteenth-century colonial Detroit transitioned to the rest of the Great Lakes. The vast inland seas that connect the Atlantic Ocean to the heart of the North American continent were fraught with perils, as observed by Kipling. An estimated ten thousand shipwrecks litter the floor of the Great Lakes. In most cases, their sinkings were of the kind associated with open water—vessels capsized by sudden storms—or the groundings and collisions seen in treacherous passages like the Straits of Mackinac or the "Doors of Death" at the mouth of Green Bay. Less spectacular, but historically a greater hazard to navigation, were the notorious St. Clair Flats, a scant twenty nautical miles above Detroit.

Characterized in an 1853 report as "the greatest natural obstacles to the free navigation of the great lakes [*sic*]," the St. Clair Flats boasts possibly the densest concentration of wreck sites in North America.[8] Here, all the waters of Lakes Superior, Michigan, and Huron, having been funneled into the St. Clair River, enter one of the world's largest freshwater deltas. In the river's pristine, unmodified state, with its velocity suddenly diminished by the proliferation of channels, the current deposits its load of suspended sediment in the form of shifting sandbars as it enters Lake St. Clair. Scene of innumerable groundings, strandings, and collisions, the waters of St. Clair system (the river, the delta, and the lake) have witnessed well over 250 sinking incidents resulting in at least 120 cases of long-term wreck site formation. Despite well over a century of dredging, towing, and

Figure 8.5 Built in Erie, Pennsylvania in 1836, the sidewheel steamer *Erie* typified navigation on the Great Lakes. In five years of service, the vessel was in two collisions, at least one grounding, and had a catastrophic boiler explosion before catching fire with great loss of life. Image courtesy of the Detroit Historical Society Collection.

demolition of obstructions by the US Army Corps of Engineers (USACE), some seventy wrecks still dot the charts between Port Huron at the head of the St. Clair River, and Belle Isle at the foot of Lake St. Clair.

The objective of this project is a spatial and temporal analysis of this dynamic environment, focusing on the century beginning with the opening of the Erie Canal in 1825. In technological terms, the nineteenth century sees multiple transitions: from sail to steam, from wooden hulls to steel. Economically, the shipping of furs and fish gives way first to timber, then to corn, wheat, coal, limestone, and iron ore, all on vast scales. New cities drive up both the supply and demand for these commodities. Lighthouses and range markers, buoys, accurate navigational charts, and weather forecasts make their appearance, all providing the means to ship more goods, faster, and more safely. While all these processes were at work throughout the Great Lakes, the distinctive transformation in the St. Clair Flats was that of the landscape itself, dredging and widening channels and harbors, forming breakwaters and seawalls, removing sandbars, snags, and other obstacles—including shipwrecks.

As a study area, the St. Clair Flats features the abundance and variety of archival information on the one hand, and the richness of the archaeological record on the other.

Regarding the former, maritime news was a staple feature of every newspaper, with arrivals, departures, and disasters reported locally. The Department of Commerce (beginning with Andrews' report of 1853), and the Lake Carriers' Association (beginning 1880) were tracking shipping: the commodities, their volume, value, and destinations. This abundance and diversity of primary sources was for many years both a blessing and a curse—definitive histories were possible, but the effort was daunting. Today, utilizing numerous databases and published research, I found myself able to compile detailed biographies of virtually every commercial vessel that reported an incident, fatal or otherwise, in the St. Clair study area during the century when most of these incidents occurred, between 1825 and 1925.

Of 130 sinkings in the St. Clair system that appear to have resulted in long-term wreck site formation, some seventy still appear on current charts, nearly fifty within the Flats and its approaches. Only about 20, or 40 percent, have been identified with any degree of certainty. The classic conundrum of the maritime archaeologist is to have a list of ships with no locations, and a chart full of wreck symbols with no names. The solution lies in using the documentation of such durable physical properties as length, beam, vessel type and construction, or evidence from the sinking incident (charred timbers, remnants of unsalvaged machinery) as diagnostics in field identification. Reuniting a wreck with its identity and biography allows the vessel to emerge as a three-dimensional entity, a whole greater than the sum of its archival record and its spot on a chart. Moreover, with a significant number of site identifications, it is possible to construct a behavioral model of the shipwrecking process in a dynamic landscape during a period of rapid and profound change in maritime technology and practice. To do this, it is also necessary to reconstruct the landscape itself.

While the St. Clair Flats has always been subject to changes by such natural processes as fluctuating lake levels, vegetation, currents, and ice jams, it is the man-made efforts of dredging and stabilization that have wrought the most profound and lasting transformation, as indexed by shipping records. In 1851, before any dredging had begun on the St. Clair River, sandbars in the Flats often reduced the effective depth of the waterway to as little as six feet. Shipping through Detroit was a mere 16,469 tons. Dredging operations commenced in 1857, and gradual improvements brought the annual tonnage to over twenty million in 1880—a volume it sustained for the following decade.[9] By 1926, the waterway was being maintained at a minimum depth of twenty feet, and increased to twenty-five feet a decade later.

Fortunately for the maritime archaeologist, the changes have been well documented through detailed official reports, surveys, and charts from the 1850s to the present. The ability to visualize and incrementally represent the evolving landscape was crucial to my effort to correlate changes in maritime practice, including post-wreck events, with the environment in which they developed.

Both the number of ships and tonnage figures increased sharply during this period, but ships continued to wreck at roughly the same rate—about three to four per year. Statistically, the Flats became safer, but fortunately left enough "time capsules" to discern some distinct pattern within the various types of wrecks.

To understand the patterns, a brief explanation of shipping trends through this period follows. Before the advent of steam, schooners negotiating the Flats under sail tended to run aground at the margins of the navigable waters. Eventually, steam towing vessels appeared to assist the sailing craft between Lakes Erie and Huron, but particularly at the Flats where local shipyards fed a thriving towboat business. Also included in the mix were steam-powered bulk freighters and passenger vessels, large and small.

Of the 286 ships reported sunk in the St. Clair system, fifty-seven (20 percent) were built along the St. Clair River: a dozen schooners, five barges, and the remaining forty steam-powered. Amid all the variables represented in the long-term wreck database, there was one constant: wooden hulls. With one exception, steel-hulled vessels were raised or salvaged. As wooden vessels aged out of the ship population, whether as schooners, barges, or steamboats, the specialized conditions that had prompted the evolution of adapted practices—short-haul towing between Lake Erie and Lake Huron—ceased to operate. Between a decline in sinkings, and the efficient salvage of the new, valuable steel hulls, long-term shipwreck site formation in the St. Clair Flats had all but ceased by 1925.

As in the case of the cannons, the wrecks can be interpreted as an assemblage. In harmony with patterns reflected in the archaeological and archival record, the full interpretive potential of multiple sites can only be realized through spatial analysis; or, more properly, multiple spatial analyses, positioning identified wrecks precisely in the landscape, and factoring each vessel's properties (e.g., vessel type, mode of propulsion, sinking incident) against the properties of its location (depth, proximity to infrastructure, or navigational hazards). Together these can provide a robust behavioral model not only of initial wreck site formation, but the long-term interaction of the maritime community with the wreck.

This is particularly productive in the case of the St. Clair Flats. Unlike deep-water wrecks that may only be relocated after many years, if at all, the wrecks of the Flats have generally remained accessible to the maritime community. Their biographies become increasingly complex, as their identity shifts from a mode of transportation to, perhaps, a navigational hazard to the mariner, a valuable resource to the salvage operator, fish habitat to the angler, a recreational opportunity to the sport diver, a source of identity to the local maritime community, and, of course, a window into the past to the historical archaeologist. Over the course of a century, a vessel may take on all these roles, and more.

In creating and interrogating my vessel database, I found broad patterns emerging almost immediately. Simply relating the nature of sinking incidents to the mode of propulsion of the sunken vessel, it became clear that, for example, capsizes (n=26) occurred to sailing vessels (n=12; 46 percent) much more frequently than to powered (n=6; 23 percent) or towed vessels (n=4; 15 percent). Collisions (n=100), on the other hand, were far more prevalent among powered vessels (n=49; 49 percent) than either sailed (n=27; 27 percent) or towed (n=16; 16 percent). Burnings (n=84), totally absent among vessels under sail, were dominated by powered vessels (n=48; 57 percent), followed by vessels immobile at their docks (n=30; 36 percent).

Adding the temporal dimension gave further depth to the analysis: while the causes of sinking were scattered throughout the study period, there was significant clustering:

capsizes peaked in the 1860s, while burnings clustered between 1877 and 1892. Collisions, always numerous, peaked in the years 1891–1910, in direct proportion to tonnage figures. Certain types of craft were seen to be more susceptible to a particular fate; as seen previously, sailing ships were prone to capsize; tugboats (n=41) account for only 14 percent of all sinkings (n=286), but a staggering 56 percent of all boiler explosions (5 out of 9).

Schooners and steamers—meet cyberspace. The toolset for integrating site data with ship biographies, and relating all to a landscape that has undergone profound alteration over years, is a Geographical Information System, or GIS. When GIS was first adopted by archaeologists in the 1980s, it was used primarily as a cartographic tool; a way to make prettier maps. The analytic possibilities have at last been embraced, as demonstrated by Price and Richards' 2009 study of multiple wreck sites in the Roanoke River.

All data for the St. Clair project, whether initially created in MS Excel, Access, or other applications (including graphics and image files), are uploaded into ESRI's ArcCatalog and managed in ArcMap. To date, I have created a geodatabase that integrates landforms, infrastructure, bathymetry of the water bodies (underwater "contour maps"), and the position of all charted wrecks in the study area. The data can be accessed and presented in many ways, most impressively as an interactive map. Where the identity and biography of a wreck is known, or onsite images and video are available, a hyperlink allows users to display, input, export, or correlate any number of details on any landscape feature, whether a wreck, a reef, a pier, or a lighthouse.

The GIS's spatial analysis tools allow the visual representation of such phenomena as in the shift in the *temporal pattern* of sinkings, as sail gave way to steam as a mode of propulsion. The dredging of the ship channel caused a shift in the *spatial pattern* from scattered shallows and sandbars, to clustered sinkings within the ship channel. This correlates to a simultaneous change in *causes*, from groundings and capsizes to collisions and fires. Clearly, to fully understand, appreciate, and interpret this complex landscape, it will be necessary to digitize not only the present submerged landscape, but its predecessors, as documented in historical charts and official reports.

An important benefit to this process is that the very features used to construct complex models of reality also allow the interpreter to create user experiences that excite as well as instruct. For example, the graphic representation of a changing submerged landscape is already familiar to the public, thanks to such television programs as the *National Geographic* channel's "Drain the Great Lakes," where animators simulate time-lapse photography to recreate glacial epochs and ancient shorelines. Thunder Bay Nation Marine Sanctuary is putting digital 3-D images of its wrecks on its website. Combining GIS with Google Maps, the Grand Traverse Bay Underwater Preserve's website features an interactive site chart featuring pop-up wreck data, photos, and sector-scan sonar images. The Lake Champlain Maritime Museum offers hands-on Remotely Operated Vehicle (ROV) user experiences aimed at school-age children, who learn to pilot the camera-equipped devices on historic wrecks.

Clearly, interactive technology, especially virtual reality, is key to contemporary interpretive strategies. The challenge lies in finding ways for the researcher, the interpreter, and the public to enter and explore that reality. Reviewing the available technology, it seems all the off-the-shelf components needed to build a "cyber-submarine" are available. Imagine a gallery simulator cruising the large-scale 3-D submerged landscape of the St. Clair Flats, the pilot inspecting 3-D wreck sites through the "viewing port," hovering over high-resolution sonar images, and, by clicking on an object in the cross-hairs, launching informational text, historical photos, narrated videos, or other interpretive content: all the data needed to conduct a sophisticated spatial analysis, plan a dive, or simply have fun while learning. Not all immersive experiences require getting wet.

Storytelling

In both cases, the objective has been to build a narrative at three levels: that of the artifact or site itself (cannon, shipwreck); that of the contextual landscape (British colonial Detroit, St. Clair Flats); and that of long-term historical events (American expansionism, industrialization, and urbanization of the Great Lakes). This is the beauty and promise of historical archaeology—to make history tangible by interpreting and reinterpreting texts, landscapes, and artifacts holistically. The credibility of the historical archaeologist's interpretation is grounded in the materiality of the evidence. I call the construction of this narrative "evidence-based storytelling." Storytelling is an ancient and honorable profession, requiring both knowledge and artistry.

It is one thing to say that the colonial interests of Great Britain and the expansionism of the United States moved inexorably toward confrontation in the strategically critical Great Lakes. It is another experience altogether to place one's hands on the cold iron of the gun, and to visualize the British troops carefully sliding it onto the treacherous river ice, determined neither to let it fall into the hands of the Americans, nor to fall in themselves. The museum visitor who may never don a scuba tank should be given the means to visualize the bustling St. Clair channel in its heyday, bristling with danger and opportunity. By building models of the past that allow us to immerse both ourselves and our audience, while never losing sight of the story, we can monitor, manage, and advocate for these irreplaceable resources, and in the end, hand the job off to a generation that is as excited and committed as we are.

Notes

1. Rudyard Kipling, *Letters of Travel 1892–1913* (New York: Doubleday, Page, 1920), 135.
2. Jonathan Adams, "Ships and Boats as Archaeological Source Material," *World Archaeology* 32, no. 3 (2001): 293.
3. John M. O'Shea and Guy A. Meadows, "Evidence for Early Hunters Beneath the Great Lakes," *Proceedings of the National Academy of Sciences*, 2009. http://www.pnas.org/content/105/25/10120.full.pdf.
4. David Nutley, "Submerged Cultural Sites: Opening a Time Capsule," *Museum International* 60, no. 4 (2008): 7–17.

5. David Gibbins and Jonathan Adams, "Shipwrecks and Maritime Archaeology," *World Archaeology* 32, no. 3 (2001): 287.

6. Guy Carleton, "Letter to John Graves Simcoe, 25 January 1796," in *Correspondence of Lieut. Governor John Graves Simcoe, with Allied Documents Relating to His Administration of the Government of Upper Canada*, Vol. 4 (Ontario Historical Society, Toronto, ON, 1923–1931), 181.

7. Daniel, Harrison, "Frontier Arms Race: Historical and Archaeological Analysis of an Assemblage of 18th-century Cannon Recovered from the Detroit River and Lake Erie," *Historical Archaeology* 48(4) (2014).

8. Israel D. Andrews, "Communication from the Secretary of the Treasury Transmitting . . . the Report of Israel D. Andrews . . . on the Trade and Commerce of the British North American Colonies, and upon the Trade of the Great Lakes and Rivers. . . ." (Washington, D.C.: Robert Armstrong, 1853), 192.

9. R. Moulton and S. Theime, *History of Dredging and Compensation: St. Clair and Detroit Rivers* (Ottawa, ON: International Upper Great Lakes Study, 2009).

CHAPTER 9

CAMPUS PRESERVATION AND SHIPWRECK RESEARCH AT WHITEFISH POINT

Bruce Lynn

HOW MANY of us remember our high school history teachers? Was it all dates and memorization for the next test? Or was that teacher the one that made history come to life?

I still remember Mr. Tucci. He made our lessons about people and the human stories behind the events in American history. As an eyewitness to the tragic confrontation at Kent State University on May 4, 1970, Tucci was able to speak with authority to a certain era of American history. And for those eras of history in which he was not actually involved, his use of primary sources and firsthand accounts allowed us all to see an event through the eyes of participants. History was more than just dates to be memorized.

Like any other subject, maritime history has the opportunity to be both captivating and painfully boring. Enthusiasts visit museums intent on learning more about a subject that is already of interest to them; depending on the intensity of enthusiasm, they may revisit the same museum or historic site over and over—or never again. Casual audiences search for destinations that entertain en route, and that entertainment can come in many forms.

The Great Lakes Shipwreck Museum occupies the site of the oldest operating light-station on Lake Superior in the remote, woodsy Eastern Upper Peninsula of Michigan. For mariners, rounding Whitefish Point was a navigational milestone. Many didn't make it, and that stretch of beach became known as the "Shipwreck Coast."

The fifty-six-acre campus includes a number of historic buildings, including a light structure, the dual lighthouse keepers' quarters, a lifeboat house and crews' dormitory, foghorn building, and auxiliary outbuildings. It is one of the most complete such installations in the world, and adjoins a US National Forest and Audubon Society bird sanctuary. Weather closes the campus during the winter months, and operations shift to winter quarters in a historic US Weather Service building in Sault Ste. Marie. Limited new construction complements the Whitefish Bay site with visitor amenities that include state-of-the-art exhibits facilities, interpretation center, archive, and gift shop.

The Shipwreck Museum interprets three main aspects of Great Lakes maritime history. The parent organization of the museum, the Great Lakes Shipwreck Historical Society (GLSHS), recently recreated their mission statement, which poetically outlines the primary areas of historical focus:

> The mission of the Great Lakes Shipwreck Historical Society is to:
> Preserve the lights and stations which warned mariners of the dangers inherent,
> Honor those who were aboard and who bravely attempted rescue and . . .
> Discover, document and interpret the vessels which instead took the deep.

The new mission statement identifies the historical focuses of the organization—lighthouse history, life-saving history, and shipwreck history. Vital to these concentrations is an active research and documentation program, and the resultant archival collection. This aspect of the museum's operations is rarely seen by the visiting public, but immediately addresses its mission. Along the Shipwreck Coast, there are hundreds of hulls lurking in the shadowy depths. In some cases, these quiet hulks are in remarkable condition—with paint intact and clearly displaying the name of a once proud vessel. Lake Superior's cold, fresh, Zebra Mussel-free waters, while challenging to navigate, provide a perfect preservative environment. For the Great Lakes Shipwreck Museum, each discovery of a new wreck opens a whole new chapter in maritime history.

The Facility

The historic light-station was abandoned by the US Coast Guard in 1970, save for the automated light which remains active today. The GLSHS was created in 1978 by a small group of teachers, historians, and scuba divers. It was very much a grassroots effort started on a modest scale, with shipwreck documentation as a primary focus. With the property came stewardship for Lighthouse Service and Life-Saving Service heritage, and the physical plant represents the organization's greatest responsibility as well as its greatest asset.

An original tower, illuminating the navigational hazards of Whitefish Point, was first lit in 1849. It was replaced by the current structure at President Abraham Lincoln's direction in 1861. The iron structure built during the Civil War still stands. It is one of the oldest light stations on the lakes and naturally serves as one of the iconic images for the museum, since it is the first thing visitors notice upon arrival. In the world of lighthouse architecture it is rather unusual on the Great Lakes. Several Atlantic Coast light structures share its iron quadrupedal, cantilevered form, but most Great Lakes lights were constructed in typical tower or house fashion, from stone quarried in the vicinity or simply from locally milled lumber. As the light is still actively maintained by the Coast Guard for navigational purposes, the tower is not accessible to visitors.

Figure 9.1 The pedestal-based tower at Whitefish Point is unusual on the Great Lakes, but the dual keepers' home is found at many of the region's hundreds of lighthouses. Photograph courtesy of Joel Stone.

Directly adjoining the light structure are the lighthouse keepers' quarters. This building is contemporary to the light structure, and has been restored to its 1890 condition. Typical of many lighthouse keepers' homes, it is conveniently bisected to accommodate both the keeper's family and that of his assistant. Each half has a well-kept parlor, dining room, and kitchen on the first floor, with two bedrooms upstairs. At this museum, the assistant keeper's home has been adapted partly for interpretation and displays, while the head keeper's dwelling has been accurately recreated to reflect the daily life of the family, complete with figures of the keeper at his desk and his wife rolling pie crusts in the kitchen. This half of the house had an assigned docent, who described the life of a lighthouse

Figure 9.2 Among the many buildings on the campus of the Great Lakes Shipwreck Museum is the reconstructed boat house, which engagingly interprets the United States Life-Saving Service's duties at this site, and the equipment they used to save stranded mariners. Photograph courtesy of Joel Stone.

keeper, discussed the artifacts on display, and pointed out the differences between the restored portions of the home and the areas preserved from the Coast Guard days.

Because Whitefish Bay was such a treacherous location, the 1923 Life-Saving Service facility consisted of three buildings—the boathouse, the crew quarters, and equipment shed. The Boathouse has been restored, and includes a replicated surfboat and beach cart, newly built to original specifications, as well as numerous artifacts and displays sponsored by various organizations and individuals. A docent is available in the boathouse to answer all questions. Notably, the facility does not include the original boathouse-to-beach railroad structure that would have been used to transport the heavy surfboat to the water. The Lifeboat Station Crew Quarters is now one of the most unique features on the campus. A beautifully rehabilitated building, it houses a bed and breakfast, opened in 2005, that operates twelve months of the year to benefit the organization. Five "themed" bedrooms are available for overnight accommodation, and offer interpretation for guests.

The main exhibitions building sits furthest from the lake, designed in a manner to complement the historic structures. The museum's main gallery is anchored by a massive second order Fresnel lens, which stands tall over the exhibits and draws the eye. An additional centerpiece is the recovered bell from the shipwreck of the 729-foot *Edmund Fitzgerald*. Over the years, the Shipwreck Museum has taken an approach that relies on

Figure 9.3 The main gallery of the Great Lakes Shipwreck Museum makes dramatic use of limited lighting, bringing to mind the fact that most shipwrecks occurred in dark, adverse conditions. A magnificent Fresnel lens, beautifully accented, anchors interpretation in this space. Photograph courtesy of Joel Stone.

static exhibits to tell the stories of shipwreck, rescue, and lighthouse life. A combination of interpretive labels, artifacts, highly detailed ship models, and original artwork/historic photographs have collectively told the dramatic stories.

The introductory display features figures representing the area's early Native inhabitants and first Europeans, as well as an explanation of the dangers of the Shipwreck Coast. Continuing around the perimeter is a chronology of thirteen wrecks explored and identified in the area. Each ship is portrayed visually by a painting or photograph, pieces of recovered deck hardware, a detailed model, and a collection of recovered relics such as dishes or personal effects. In addition, there is a paragraph or two describing the circumstances of each ship's foundering, and a small map showing the location of the remains. These ship portraits are all presented in the same format, which allows for ease of comprehension and comparison. The backgrounds of the units vary in color, making each one distinct, and adding vibrancy to the otherwise dark exhibit hall.

The shipwrecks are arranged in chronological order, going as far back as 1816 and as recent as 1975, in the *Fitzgerald*'s case. An eerie sound track (Brian Eno, *Music for Films*)

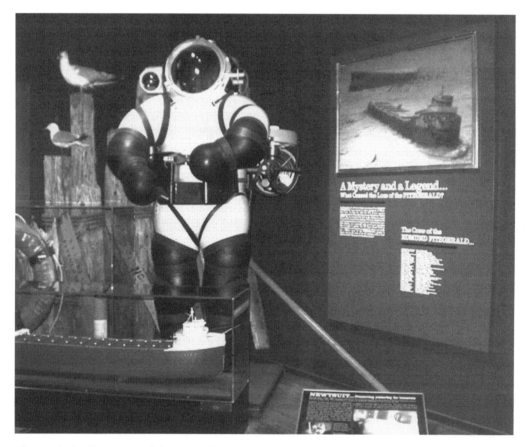

Figure 9.4 The story of the SS *Edmund Fitzgerald* is a significant part of the attraction at Whitefish Point, and the museum dedicates appropriate space. This hard-shell diving suit was used to transfer ceremonial bells to and from the *Fitz*'s foredeck. Photograph courtesy of Joel Stone.

pervades the gallery, while lighting is strictly controlled. This combination of objects, human narratives, and images does an impressive job of captivating the visitor. In one corner of the gallery, remnants of an actual ship hull lie quietly while realistic scuba divers hover overhead, speaking to the methodology for shipwreck documentation. The delicate balance of ambient light, sound, and objects encourages reflection and hushed tones on the part of museum visitors. Special attention is paid to the brevity of each label. While much more could be told, available space in the gallery and summer visitation numbers dictate otherwise. During a mid-summer day, it is not uncommon to see eight hundred to one thousand people walking though the gallery.

Interpretation

In recent years, the challenge of updating the exhibits in the main gallery has been a dilemma. How to complement the existing balance, without taking away from those elements which make it such an effective and captivating space? The existing exhibits do an excellent job of capturing the *human stories* of so many tragic situations. They subtly reminded visitors that these dramatic stories occurred, in many cases, just off the beach outside of the museum.

What could be added? What might be missing? Two answers stood out: this exhibit needs to represent the sheer volume of wrecks throughout the Great Lakes; and it needs to take visitors to places that few would ever see. New technology, paid for in part by a grant from the Michigan Humanities Council, allowed the viewing of high-definition underwater footage of the process of exploring a shipwreck. It was critical to make these new elements blend seamlessly with the existing space and not create traffic bottlenecks.

The next question became which shipwrecks to include? It was felt that to truly be the Great Lakes Shipwreck Museum, it would be appropriate to include ships that had come to grief on *any* of the Great Lakes. Two opportunities immediately presented themselves.

At the time in 2011, two shipwreck survivors were semifrequent visitors to the museum. Their shipwrecks were more recent than most of the vessels represented in the exhibit, having occurred in 1958 and 1966. New panels were created to include these newer wrecks, and two small monitors were incorporated into the area showing extraordinary underwater footage of the *Carl D. Bradley* and the *Daniel J. Morrell*. This is complemented by historic photographs and footage showing each ship in their glory days, which blended nicely with the existing exhibits. In each case, the videos are relatively short in duration and feature no audio.

The interpretive magic happened when the two survivors came to the exhibit to tell their stories. The late Dennis Hale, sole survivor of the 1966 *Daniel J. Morrell* shipwreck, spoke to a large crowd in the main gallery during the summer of 2012. He told his story to a diverse group, with ages ranging from elementary school children to senior citizens. Hale's story was one of tragedy, as twenty-nine of his fellow crewmen perished with their ship. He survived thirty-eight hours on a life raft in freezing conditions. As the saying goes, one could hear a pin drop as he recounted his experiences. Frank Mays, one of two

Figure 9.5 Dennis Hale, sole survivor of the *Daniel J. Morrell* sinking in 1966, was always welcome at the Great Lakes Shipwreck Museum. Mr. Hale died in 2015. Photograph courtesy of the Great Lakes Shipwreck Museum.

survivors of the 1958 *Carl D. Bradley* shipwreck, told *his* story during the summer of 2015. The crowd was transfixed.

Live, first-person recollections can be spellbinding and informative, adding perspective to the known facts and characters. Most people willing to tell their stories have positive presentation skills, but not always. When people discuss tragedies, the narrative can be unpredictable. This shouldn't deter this type of presentation, but understand the emotions and sensitivities in the room.

Each spring, the Great Lakes Shipwreck Museum welcomes thousands of schoolchildren through its doors. It is enjoyable interacting with the kids as they clamor through the historic structures—seeing what catches their eye. Engaging them in lighthouse history, though, can be a challenge. In some cases, the teachers have introduced the students to certain aspects of maritime history and there is a basic understanding. The campus makes it easier to understand. For the uninitiated, we just start from a different spot, historically.

The greatest interpretive opportunity comes when student groups spend the night at Whitefish Point Station. Special evening programs allow museum staff to try out new interpretive ideas with the group and have some fun at the same time. Interactive programs have worked well in such situations. One program, as an example, introduces the study of lighthouse "characteristics" and why lighthouses look the way they do, both day and night. At the onset of the program, the museum staff asks for volunteers and

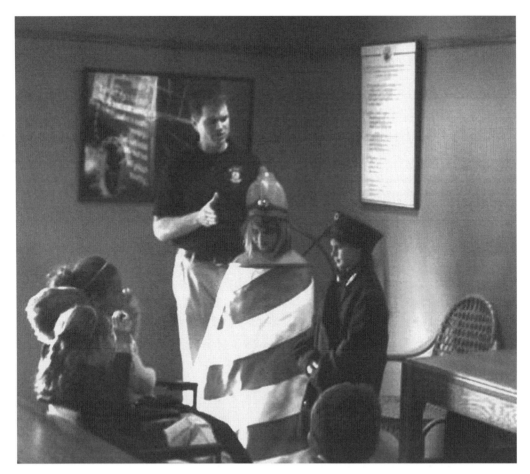

Figure 9.6 A class lesson about how lighthouses communicate with ships becomes interactive when students are assigned duties as lighthouse keeper and the lighthouse. Photograph courtesy of the Great Lakes Shipwreck Museum.

picks two students, one of whom is turned into a lighthouse. This is accomplished by a wraparound costume that transforms the student into a colorful lighthouse. The simple act of turning the student into a lighthouse elicits a comedic reaction for the remaining students and garners everybody's attention. A hat, with an adjustable head-lamp and red/clear colors, represents the lighthouse lantern room. The second student becomes a lighthouse keeper, with a youth-sized keeper uniform, and both are sequestered for instruction.

The rest of the group sees a PowerPoint presentation introducing a variety of lighthouses and their various light signaling systems, including flash timing and colors. Then, the student "lighthouse" and keeper are brought back into view and worksheets with different lighthouse flash and color characteristics are handed out. At the front of the room the keeper creates light signals via the headlamp, each light signal corresponding with a lighthouse on the worksheet. The students watch intently to see what combination of colors and duration will come next. It is as if they are seeing the lighthouse at night from a ship. Such programs have worked well at the Great Lakes Shipwreck Museum with smaller groups and in classroom settings.

The museum's interpretive approach is constantly under review. Discussions with fellow museum professionals weigh the effectiveness of programs and exhibitions overall. They center on the changing expectations of museum guests; quietly walking through a museum gallery and reading text labels is not for everybody. Young visitors and parents with children have pointed out over the years that the museum features no interactive components. In 2013 an installation initiative created a relatively simple exhibition incorporating hands-on components, appealing to youth and adults alike. Discussions at the staff level, adhering to the GLSHS mission, focused on such famous shipwrecks as the *Griffon* and the *Edmund Fitzgerald*, representing the first and last major shipwrecks on the Great Lakes.

The *Fitzgerald* became a centerpiece in the new exhibit through a masterful recreation of the famous ship in LEGO form. The twelve-foot-long model, comprised of over eighteen thousand LEGO pieces, commands attention and draws youngsters like a magnet. Adjacent to this model is a medium-sized table, where thousands of LEGO pieces allow visitors to build their own ship models. Parents and children alike sit in the smallish chairs and build—then often wreck—their own ships. An exhibit panel explains how the LEGO model started as a high school class project, designed to instruct the students about shipping on the Great Lakes.

Another component encourages youngsters and adults to identify maritime artifacts and draw them on a chalkboard table. A small steam engine, representative of early freighter engines, can be "fired up," with young guests pulling a small chain to activate the "steam" whistle. Most elements of the exhibition are at a child's eye level.

In a scenario experienced by museum folks across the country, one very popular part of the exhibit, similar to a video game, allowed museum guests to navigate a busy Great Lakes port and gather cargo along the way. Unfortunately, this software-driven component was prone to technical problems. After several months, a face cut-out mural replaced it, providing an equally popular photo opportunity, and contains no moving parts.

Programming is an important part of the facility's appeal. Tours, concerts, fish boils, lectures, and publications add depth to Whitefish Point's static offerings, and draw enthusiastic visitors. Among the most significant, mission-driven events is the annual postseason Memorial Ceremony which takes place on November 10—the anniversary of the SS *Edmund Fitzgerald* sinking. Family members of the crew, and those from similar tragedies, are usually present to share their stories, insights, and comfort.

Due to its remote location, the Whitefish Point campus is closed from November through April. During this time the GLSHS retreats to the former USDA Weather Bureau building adjacent to the Soo Locks in Sault Ste. Marie. Built in 1899, the structure was restored by the Society, and provides office, archive, and interpretive space during winter months. The GLSHS maintains the research vessel *David Boyd* to support its archaeological mission, and offers numerous video and text material, on the website www.shipwreckmuseum.com.

The museum relies primarily on admissions revenue for its operations, and benefits from a destination tourism coupled to the Soo Locks, Tahquamenon Falls, and other local lighthouses. The on-site bed and breakfast in the Crew's Quarters, an extensive museum store with food service, and special ticketed lighthouse tower climbs supplement operating revenue. These revenue streams, combined with a successful development program allow for ongoing historic preservation efforts. A combination of purpose-built museum buildings and historic structures blend together nicely, offering a unique visitor experience.

Similarly, old and new organizations partner to ensure the future of this corner of the world. A joint committee of land holding partners—which includes the US Fish and Wildlife Service through the Seney National Wildlife Refuge, the Michigan Audubon Society at the Whitefish Point Bird Observatory, and the Shipwreck Society—governs changes and development on the site overall, while the Michigan State Historic Preservation office is consulted on all changes/updates to the historic structures.

Conclusion

The fascination of this Lake Superior site is that "it happened here." Stories are best told and best understood when related *in situ*. Along the Shipwreck Coast there are thousands of stories that fit Mr. Tucci's curricula—within these wrecks are the primary accounts, *the* primary source. Every boat that fought through storm and fog for safe passage around Whitefish Point—relying on the Whitefish Point Station—has a story. Those stories are told here.

CHAPTER 10

CURATING AND EXHIBITING RECREATIONAL BOATING

John Summers

I F YOU WERE to ask a visitor to a maritime museum or historic ship to name important themes in North American maritime history, it is reasonable to expect that they would mention at least some of the topics that make up the chapters in this book: whaling, naval affairs, shipwrecks, commercial shipping, lighthouses, and inland waterways. It is also reasonable to expect that far fewer, if any, would mention the fiberglass runabout on its trailer in their driveway, or the personal watercraft at their vacation house. Yet pleasure boating is and has been an activity of significant economic and social consequence, and is worthy of consideration as an important part of maritime history.

But it's only pleasure! How could it possibly be as serious a topic as the navy, or exploration, or shipping? In the words of naval architect and historian Douglas Phillips-Birt, from his book *An Eye for a Yacht*,

> Yachting was as exclusive, as brilliant, as undemocratic as a Florentine palace. And it was creative. Some of the most original and talented minds in several countries devoted themselves to the creation of the yachting fleets—men who might have reached the top in any sphere of imaginative work.[1]

The high net-worth individuals who commissioned grand yachts from designers such as the Herreshoffs, C. Raymond Hunt, Clinton Crane, Starling Burgess, and Olin Stephens were no less patrons of genius than the Renaissance princes who brought out the best work in the artists they supported. Their choices, exercised free of almost all of the constraints that normally bind you and me, are therefore a truer index of desire than many more pragmatic and workaday decisions.

This is just as true at lower levels of expenditure. Pleasure craft, like automobiles, are vehicles of aspiration, and their selection and purchase speaks as much, if not more, to who we wish to be than who we are. Yachting and pleasure boating, whether for recreation or racing, can be as much about social performance as performance on the water, and the clubs, burgees, races, uniforms, and handicapping rules of organized sport can offer insights into social as well as maritime history.

The mass-market builders of recreational boats such as Chris-Craft, Lyman, and the Peterborough-area canoe companies were economic pillars of their respective communities and regions, shipping their products around the world. In more recent times the collection and preservation of such pleasure craft has also become a major economic activity. In the last fifty years, a very short span of time in the overall sweep of maritime history, old pleasure and working craft have been transformed from something that was likely to be found at the end of the driveway to be picked up with the trash to a "hobby" so significant that a whole sector of service industries has grown up around it. The antique boat industry today sustains a legion of restorers, suppliers, and builders of new boats in the classic style, and new market segments, such as specialized insurance coverage, have been developed expressly for it. Four events have fostered this interest in our recreational boating heritage.

In 1964, a group of friends in the 1000 Islands region of the St. Lawrence River got together to celebrate the preservation and restoration of their wooden boats. Encouraged by the interest shown by the public, they resolved to meet again the following summer. More than fifty years later, the Antique Boat Museum in Clayton, New York, which evolved out of these annual boat shows, still hosts a show each summer and hundreds of similar events take place across the United States and Canada annually. The museum has prospered, and now holds the largest collection of recreational watercraft in the world.

In 1974, a young man living in a teepee in the Maine woods named Jonathan Wilson started an unlikely magazine entirely devoted to wooden boats which he called, appropriately enough, *The Wooden Boat*. *Wooden Boat* magazine (they dropped the definite article in their early years) has published more than 250 bimonthly issues and created a renowned school and an extensive publishing empire, all run from its home base in the seaside hamlet of Brooklin, Maine.

In 1975, a group of antique pleasure boating enthusiasts got together in Boston, Massachusetts, and formed the Antique and Classic Boat Society, "dedicated to bringing together people with a love of antique and classic boats and boating." Today the ACBS has more than fourteen thousand members who together own many times that number of antique and classic boats and belong to both the parent organization and one of more than fifty-five chapters in the United States, Canada, and France.

In the 1950s, educator, boatbuilder, and historian John Gardner began writing for *The National Fisherman*. Drawing on years of accumulated knowledge and the wealth of examples preserved in museum collections, Gardner's articles showed how traditional small craft could be brought to life again as recreational boats. Almost more importantly than reviving the designs themselves, he encouraged prospective owners to consider building their own boat, and wrote a series of now-classic books about traditional boatbuilding. In the mid-1970s he began teaching boatbuilding at Mystic Seaport Museum, and his pioneering efforts sparked a renaissance of interest in amateur boatbuilding.

The history of pleasure boating is the history of the gradual democratization of access to the water for recreation, but before there was recreational boating, there was yachting, and yachting's origins are unabashedly royal. In 1660 King Charles II was presented with a small Dutch pleasure vessel of a type known as a "Jaght." The Duke of York was so taken with the King's little ship that he ordered a similar one built and thus the first yacht race took place almost as soon as there were two yachts on the water. Although the New York Yacht Club was founded in 1844 and the schooner *America* won the trophy that was to bear her name in 1851, American yachting did not come to broad public notice until after the end of the Civil War when the first two challenges for the Cup took place in the United States in 1870 and 1871.

The Scottish barrister John MacGregor was a peripatetic adventurer and muscular Christian who, beginning in 1865, traveled the length and breadth of Europe in a series of small canoes called *Rob Roy*. His accounts of these travels, beginning in 1866 with *A Thousand Miles in the Rob Roy Canoe*, were immensely popular and went through many editions. He also gave lectures and exhibited his canoes. In 1858 MacGregor had traveled through the United States and Canada and paddled bark and dugout canoes. He had also reportedly encountered aboriginal skin-on-frame watercraft in an earlier trip to Siberia. He took his impressions back to Europe with him and commissioned the boatbuilders Searle and Sons in Lambeth on the Thames to build him a new boat.

Marrying up the slim, double-ended form of aboriginal watercraft with European-style lapstrake boatbuilding, Searle produced a sturdy fifteen-foot-long, partially decked boat, made principally of oak and weighing eighty pounds. Christened *Rob Roy* in honor of his Scottish outlaw ancestor and the leading figure in Walter Scott's eponymous three-volume novel, the new boat was a true hybrid, an intercultural mixture of European and aboriginal boatbuilding. Known as a "double-paddle canoe," she was heavier than

Figure 10.1 Double-paddle canoes and cruising sailing canoes inspired by MacGregor's *Rob Roy* were the original "personal watercraft." This 1888 tobacco card appeals to canoeists. Image courtesy of the author.

skin-on-frame kayaks but much more durable. Like them, the boat was propelled with a double-bladed paddle. Mostly decked over, the cockpit was made waterproof with a rubberized apron which the canoeist placed in his lap, though unlike the kayak, she was not designed to be rolled.

MacGregor's intrepid independence matched well with the ideas of Victorian society and his exploits inspired legions of paddlers and canoe travelers and the formation of the Royal Canoe Club (founded in 1866/received royal warrant in 1874), the New York Canoe Club (1871), and the American Canoe Association (1880). Canoeing blossomed into the first widespread recreational pastime and this popularity endured until it was supplanted by bicycling at the end of the nineteenth century.

Competitive rowing had existed as a spectator sport since the early years of the nineteenth century, when thousands watched and large sums were wagered on the outcome of races between professional watermen and oarsmen. A crowd of more than one hundred thousand are said to have seen Toronto, Ontario's Edward "Ned" Hanlan defeat Australia's Edward Trickett for the championship of the world on the Thames in November 1880. Amateur rowing was also popular, and clubs and boathouses could be found on lakes, rivers, coastlines, and college campuses throughout North America. Providence, Rhode Island's Narragansett Boat Club, founded in 1838, claims the title as America's oldest continuously operating rowing club.

The history of recreational boating cannot be told without also inquiring into the history of leisure time and the idea of the vacation. Just as the concept of zero, so embedded in our lives today as to be entirely taken for granted, had to be invented (or discovered, depending on your point of view), so too did the idea of free time need to be converted from a temptation sent by the devil to a goal to be pursued and cherished.

It is no accident that the great popularity of John MacGregor's canoeing voyages occurred at the end of the first Industrial Revolution. Recreational boating needed the new technologies of this era and the wealth and aspirations of its rising middle class to flourish, and both were provided by the mechanical transformation of the western world. If you labored long hours for six or more days a week, your time for going on the water was of necessity limited. Rising affluence and changes in the structure of labor brought about a new middle class that had both time for recreation and the means with which to pursue it.

If writers and pundits were decrying the noisome atmosphere of the cities in which you made your wages and encouraging you to seek out the wilderness to refresh your mind and body, and if there was a railway line to take you out of the city, and if there was a hotel carved out of the forest by a sparkling lake at the end of the line, then you might also be in want of a boat. In your pocket there might be a copy of a heavily illustrated railway timetable extolling the virtues of your destination. You could also have been inspired by a volume such as outdoorsman George Washington Sears' *Woodcraft* or Adirondack promoter W. H. H. Murray's *Adventures in the Wilderness,* or be a subscriber to one of the new sporting journals such as *Forest and Stream* or *The Aquatic Monthly and Nautical Review.*

In New York State's Adirondack Park, in the St. Lawrence River's 1000 Islands, and in the Muskoka area of southern Ontario, hotels and boat rental liveries arose to cater

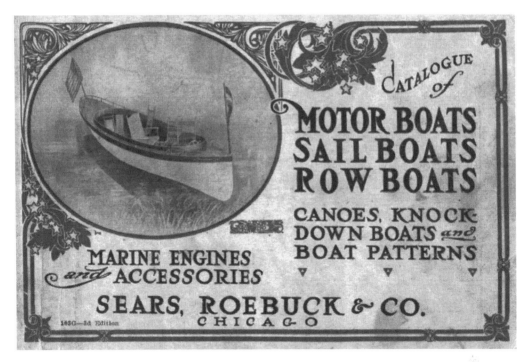

Figure 10.2 Department store retailers such as Sears were quick to see the potential market in recreational boating and the company offered a range of boats and boating products through both their catalogs and stores. This image is from the 1907 Sears, Roebuck & Company catalog, courtesy of the Antique Boat Museum.

to these new vacationers. Each of these destinations produced its own type or types of recreational boats. The frequent portages, or "carries," as they were known locally in the Adirondacks, placed a premium on lightness of construction, and so the area became known both for lightweight lapstrake canoes such as those produced by Canton's J. Henry Rushton, and for the Adirondack Guideboat, a unique rowing craft that could also be easily carried between bodies of water.

The more exposed and rougher waters of the mighty St. Lawrence River gave rise to the St. Lawrence Skiff, a seaworthy and easily driven rowing and sailing skiff used by professional guides to take their "sports" out fishing. The many lakes of the Muskoka region a short distance north of Toronto fostered a unique boating culture and were home to noted builders such as Greavette, Minette, and Ditchburn. The submerged granite rocks in their Canadian Shield waters also helped to create distinctive local types such as the Disappearing Propeller Boat, whose universal-jointed shaft would rise up into the hull when it struck an obstacle.

Steam engines were being placed in pleasure craft by the last quarter of the nineteenth century but in the United States they required a licensed engineer to operate. A more accessible, albeit hazardous-sounding, alternative was the naphtha engine, fitted into the same type of long, narrow launch hull. These engines worked by boiling and condensing naphtha, a petroleum distillate similar to gasoline, which also fed the burner that heated the liquid. Despite how alarming it sounds, boiling gasoline was relatively safe, and naphtha launches were a common sight (and sound, with the roaring noise of their pressurized burners) on North American waterways into the early twentieth century.

Boating did not have to stop in the winter months of the year. The first iceboats are recorded in seventeenth-century Holland and were in use in North America by the early nineteenth century. Long before the advent of high-speed trains and cars, iceboats carried their skippers and crews for thrilling rides at well over one hundred miles per hour.

The most significant democratization of pleasure boating occurred with the creation of the outboard motor in the twentieth century. Though low-powered, heavy, and difficult to operate by modern standards, these early "detachable rowboat motors," as they were styled by one manufacturer, prompted a revolution in hull design and opened boating up to a much wider audience. As in other areas of pleasure boating, it wasn't long before the new outboard motors were being used for racing, and the pressures of competition drove technical developments that were soon reflected in consumer products as manufacturers showcased their racing successes. Antique outboard motors today are a popular and affordable sector of the antique boat hobby.

Driven by rapid advances in inboard and outboard engine technology, the early years of the twentieth century witnessed a rapid expansion of recreational boating. As inboard engines became more powerful and reliable, long narrow launch hulls gave way to beamier planing runabouts and some of the most famous pleasure boat marques were born. Detroiter Garfield Arthur "Gar" Wood used his industrial fortune to fund his powerboat racing hobby, and then parlayed his racing successes into a line of recreational runabouts bearing his name that are today some of the most sought-after of all antique boats. Christopher Columbus Smith also turned racing victories into commercial success as he and his brothers built Chris-Craft into a pleasure boat empire that produced hulls ranging in size from rowing prams to substantial cabin cruisers.

On the waters of the Great Lakes, the Lyman company produced sturdy lapstrake hulls popular with fishermen. Based in Sandusky, Ohio, their refined production methods, which used patterns for every single part of the boat, helped them to rapidly manufacture extraordinary numbers of wooden hulls. Builders such as Elco and Matthews produced substantial power craft and east and west coast yards such as Herreshoff, Nevins, Trumpy, and Kettenburg built significant yachts.

The peacetime activity of recreational boating benefitted significantly from warfare and conflict. Boatbuilding yards and factories were converted to war production to produce landing craft, PT boats, pontoons, and floating bridges. Yachts were offered by their owners for service as coastal patrol craft. Following the First World War, surplus aircraft engines such as the Liberty were purchased in great numbers by builders such as Gar Wood. Converted for marine use, their high power to weight ratios revolutionized powerboat racing. After the Second World War, supercharged Rolls-Royce and Allison aircraft engines drove a new generation of racing hydroplanes. New materials such as molded plywood and aluminum, and surplus wartime production capacity, were put to use in manufacturing thousands of durable and inexpensive new boats for a rapidly expanding market.

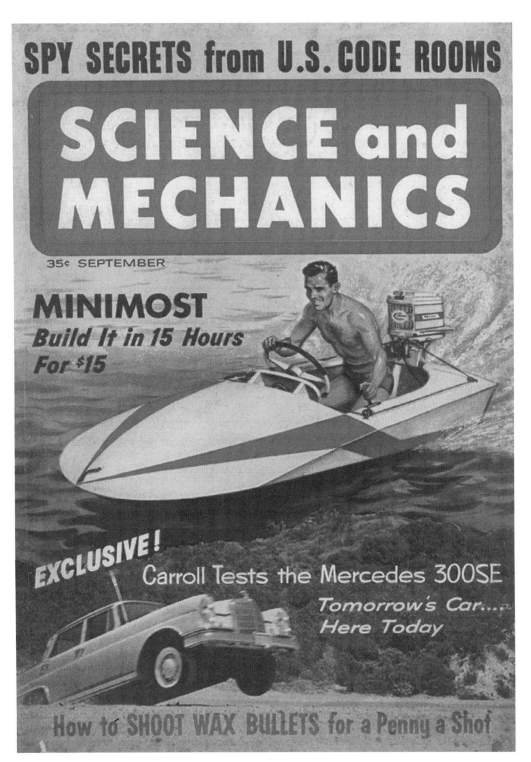

Figure 10.3 Since the earliest days of pleasure boating in North America, kits, plans, and instructions have encouraged a do-it-yourself attitude toward getting on the water. Outboard hydroplane designs such as the Minimost are still a popular and accessible part of the pastime today. This image is from the September 1962 *Science and Mechanics* magazine, courtesy of the author.

Experimenters like Gar Wood's son Gar Wood Jr. made the first tentative forays into resin and cloth composite hulls during the war but it wasn't until the development of polyester resins in 1942 that fiberglass cloth, which had existed since the early 1930s, could be combined with it into a sturdy boat hull material that could be molded into virtually any shape.

Boats and cars had been linked since the "autoboats" of the earliest days of powerboating, so-called because they featured automobile-style seating and driving arrangements and used automotive components and engines. The major pleasure boat manufacturers maintained networks of dealerships organized along the lines of automobile sales organizations, and their catalogs featured annual model and styling changes like cars. The advent of fiberglass technology in the years following World War II allowed boats and cars to converge stylistically as well. Intoxicated by their ability to mold any shape they wanted, and perhaps concerned more with styling and novelty than technical performance, manufacturers began to add automotive-style features such as hard tops, tail fins, and tail lights to their boats. Today these so-called fiberglassics are one of the fastest-growing segments of the antique boating hobby.

Over the broad sweep of recreational boating history, several developments stand out as game-changers. As noted earlier, the outboard motor was a pivotal technology

Figure 10.4 The history of recreational boating is an anatomy of desire and longing. This image is from a 1958 Evinrude brochure, courtesy of the Antique Boat Museum.

that changed boating forever. The inexpensive, durable, and mass-produced aluminum canoe of the 1950s not only brought canoeing to a wider audience but also fostered new segments of the sport such as whitewater canoeing as paddlers banged their way down previously un-runnable rapids with scant regard for their easily repaired metal canoes.

Just after the end of the Second World War, surfer Woody Brown built a catamaran in Hawaii called *Manu Kai*. Fast and lightweight, this modern evocation of traditional Polynesian voyaging canoes inspired other designers such as Rudy Choy, who created large cruising and racing catamarans, and surfboard builder Hobie Alter, who designed the Hobie Cat and sparked widespread interest in multihulls. Newman Darby, Peter Chilvers, Jim Drake, and Hoyle Schweitzer all share credit for creating and popularizing the sailboard, popularly known as a "windsurfer." Drake and Schweitzer were awarded a patent for their sailboard in 1970.

C. Raymond Hunt's and Dick Fisher's 1958 thirteen-foot Boston Whaler, with its stable and unsinkable foam-filled "cathedral" hull, was immediately successful and is still in production. Hunt's deep-V hull shape, made famous by Dick Bertram's series of *Moppie* offshore racing powerboats, is today the standard hull form for recreational and racing powerboats alike. The Alcort "board boat" Sailfish and Sunfish designs, with their distinctive lateen sails, were fun, wet, and easy to sail and this, combined with their portability and low price, brought many new sailors into the sport. Canadian Bruce Kirby's 1971 Laser sailboat offered the same accessible experience in a more performance-oriented boat. The personal watercraft of the early 1970s, beginning with Kawasaki's "Jet Ski," are now ubiquitous on inland and coastal waters.

Recreational boating has a great deal of interpretive potential within the broad scope of maritime history. North America's maritime museums hold large collections of historic recreational boats and archival materials. While the boats themselves are interesting and sometimes spectacular in their own right, the exhibits in which they are placed can sometimes appeal more to specialists than a broader audience. Some of the challenges of curating and interpreting pleasure boating history are common to all museums that deal with the history of technology. Displayed without context as objects of pure art-for-arts'-sake connoisseurship, technological artifacts such as antique boats and automobiles can become fetish objects. While collectors and those in the know may appreciate this visible-storage style of exhibition, such a bare-bones approach can leave visitors with no prior knowledge or only a general interest in the topic, out in the cold (or standing on the dock).

It can sometimes be difficult to accommodate both specialist and generalist interests within the same display. In the early 2000s, the Antique Boat Museum developed a new exhibit featuring its extensive collection of antique outboard motors. The motors were paired with many boats from the collection and displayed in groupings interspersed with large graphics taken from archival advertising material. Titled "Outboards! The Motors That Changed Pleasure Boating," the exhibit was intended to provide an accessible glimpse into both the emergence of this boating technology and the museum's collections. While popular with the general public, this style of presentation also provoked a strong response from some outboard collectors, who were irritated that the motors weren't "properly" displayed. For them, this meant grouped by manufacturer and ranked by year of production, as they would be for judging at an antique boat show.

The same connoisseurship-driven approach can lead to such artifacts being over-restored and presented in a condition far better than that in which they originally left the showroom. Judging at enthusiasts' shows and "concours" events can privilege perfection over reality, and result in original fabric with historical and evidentiary value being discarded in favor of a flawless, one-hundred-point appearance. This issue has been addressed in recent years, and antique and classic boats can now be judged both on their degree of preservation and restoration, though there is still a strong tendency to make them look better than the day they were made.

It is tempting to present the history of technology as the history of inevitable forward progress and focus on achievements and successes at the expense of a fuller consideration of the story. This is an important point for exhibit-making in history and technology museums. Presenting a beautiful, over-restored artifact as the epitome of achievement (this is the boat that won the race; this is the Wright brothers' airplane) can obscure more interesting parts of the story, and make success appear inevitable. If such pinnacles of achievement are lined up next to each other in gleaming rows, a modality of display common in automotive museums, celebration can triumph over analysis.

This is not to say that we and our visitors shouldn't cherish beauty or achievement for their own sake—see, for instance, a chapter of Phillips-Birt's book almost entirely devoted to the psychological impact of various kinds of curves as they are used in yacht sheerlines—but rather that we should be alive to the history of failure as well as success, and endeavor to work backward from the artifacts in our museums to present their cultural and historical contexts to visitors.

For example, an exhibit of racing powerboats from the early years of the twentieth century that competed in the annual Gold Cup race could support (at least) a history of the naval architecture of the planing hull, an introduction to basic principles of physics, the story of the development of the internal combustion engine, the achievements of the designers of aircraft powerplants, and the sciences of aerodynamics and hydrodynamics.

In 2007 the Antique Boat Museum began development of a new exhibit about powerboat racing. For some years previously, the museum had been in possession of both a collection of historic racing powerboats and engines and a building in which to display them, but the exhibit had consisted of a basic "boats-in-a-row" style of presentation with only minimal interpretive material. In that year the decision was taken to upgrade this presentation into a full-fledged educational exhibit to be called "Quest for Speed: The Story of Powerboat Racing." The building that was to house the exhibit posed some challenges. A large rectangular structure of just over six thousand square feet, it was of timber-frame construction, three stories to the peak of the roof and with a narrow second-floor mezzanine running down one side. Large windows on one side and in both ends flooded the building with light, and the interior walls were clad in white-stained knotty hemlock.

The principal design and curatorial challenge was to create an exhibit that would engage two distinct audiences: the walk-in visitors who flocked to this resort community

Figure 10.5 The "Quest for Speed: The Story of Powerboat Racing" exhibition is a nicely textured exhibit that makes the most of its facility. The balance of beautiful boats and pertinent information "about both the boats and the people who drove them" satisfies both the enthusiast and neophyte. Photograph courtesy of the Antique Boat Museum.

during the summer season and the committed enthusiasts and collectors who came to the museum's biennial Antique Raceboat Regatta and its annual antique boat show. The museum had a long tradition of displaying the boats in its collection with minimal interpretive material, a modality some staff called the "indoor boat show." The ambition for this new exhibit was to provide a full and engaging interpretive and educational experience and to introduce the stories of people who designed, built, owned, and drove the boats to enhance the interpretation of the boats themselves. In so doing it was hoped that the high-information collectors, connoisseurs, and raceboat enthusiasts would find satisfyingly detailed information and a true reflection of the sport they loved. The tourists and walk-in visitors would discover a popular and accessible introduction to the world of fast and beautiful racing powerboats.

For one of the long interior walls, a timeline was developed that showed milestones in the world water speed record. The longitudinal axis gave the year and boat of each new record, and the vertical axis showed steadily rising speeds. Each boat and engine had its own dashboard panel with a narrative description and detailed technical information. Boats were displayed on custom-made timber cradles, and higher-freeboard boats had accessible ramps to allow a glimpse into the cockpits. Each boat was also pitched up a few degrees at the bow which helped to animate the view across the exhibit floor.

Figure 10.6 Seeking to broaden the scope of its exhibit offerings, the Canadian Canoe Museum created the "Can I Canoe You Up the River?" exhibition, which explored the popular culture association between canoes and romance. Exhibit design element courtesy of the Canadian Canoe Museum, based on a postcard in the collection of the author.

A series of freestanding interpretive panels called "Speed Kings" and "Speed Queens" presented photos and biographies of leading powerboat racers. Racing outboard hydroplanes were cantilevered from the balcony so that they could be seen from above and below, and one hydroplane was suspended from the ceiling. Below the mezzanine, large glassed-in showcases displayed racing souvenirs and memorabilia and racing equipment such as helmets and lifejackets. Large freestanding video monitors displayed edited loops of racing footage, a dramatic sequence from *Magnificent Obsession* starring Rock Hudson and Jane Wyman, and *Racing Fever*, a lurid 1950s B movie about hydroplanes. Additional popular culture flavor was provided by a working 1980s "Hydro Thunder" arcade game and a dime-store kiddie ride in the shape of an offshore raceboat. Coin boxes on these two elements were left at twenty-five cents per use, and signage promised that proceeds would be used to care for the museum's collections.

Several years later, the Canadian Canoe Museum took a similar curatorial approach. The museum has a rich and remarkable collection of more than six hundred canoes, kayaks, and paddled watercraft. Established in Peterborough in 1997, its long-term exhibits explore the cornerstones of the canoe in Canada, including the fur trade, northern exploration, aboriginal cultures, and the Peterborough-area canoe builders. A changing exhibit space allows the annual presentation of additional topics. In 2012, the museum began to create a new social history exhibit for this space. It would draw on a major assemblage of canoeing-themed postcards recently acquired from a private collector.

An American member of the Wooden Canoe Heritage Association also owned a remarkable collection of so-called courting canoes and was willing to lend some of them for exhibit. Together with another private collection of canoeing ephemera and the museum's own artifact and archival holdings, these offered the opportunity to explore the theme of canoes and romance. A new volume in the museum's recently initiated series of Gallery Guide publications would also serve as the exhibit's catalog. Called "Can I Canoe You Up the River," the resulting exhibit blended popular songs, advertising, and postcard graphics and the beautiful courting canoes themselves, fitted out with parasols, pillows, and gramophones to allow visitors to uncover an important popular culture aspect of the canoe's history.

From the designs and technologies embodied in the boats themselves to the social and cultural aspects of their use and enjoyment, the preservation and interpretation of the artifacts and archives of recreational boating can yield rich insight into the broader themes of maritime history. From the humble fisherman's rowing skiff to the plutocrat's yacht, the vehicles of desire in which we take to the water to relax, socialize, compete, and simply enjoy being afloat have much to tell us about who we are, who we have been, and who we wish to be.

Note

1. Douglas Phillips-Birt, *An Eye for a Yacht* (London: Faber & Faber, 1955), 13–14.

CHAPTER 11

LIVING MARITIME HISTORY

Chanties, Ballads, and Folktales

Joel Stone, with Lee Murdock and Joann Murdock

MUSIC OF the maritime world is important because it is generally fun, often dramatic, and reaches an audience as broad as the topic; nearly every type of museum, website, and live gathering utilizes music to set a mood and teach a tradition. American maritime music has its own unique soundtrack, which serves as both an entertainment and experiential tool, and an incredible window into the lives of people who made their living in a water-dependent economy. Songs by and about sailors are likely as old as the profession, and are part of folk song traditions on every continent. Working songs of the American maritime—chanties or shanties—are traced to the mid-fourteenth century, European sea trade, and were actively in service until the early twentieth century.

Singing traditions of the colonial American sailor were seamlessly drawn from the British Isles, but are indelibly global. Because of strong American interaction with commercial trade routes across the Atlantic and to Asia, there are also traces of German, Mediterranean, west African, and Polynesian idioms to be found. French and Native American tunes mixed across the northern frontier and down the Mississippi. There likely were times on North America's West Coast when Spanish voices met Russian, Yankee, and Native. Not all their songs were about work, but the chanted cadences of hauling tunes were invaluable for communication, efficiency, and morale.[1]

Melodies about sailors come in all forms. Ballads eulogized great admirals, memorialized battles, and praised crack, efficient vessels. More often poor Sailor Jack is the subject of endless travails, adventures, odd turns, and tragedies, both ashore and at sea. Favorite ships, hated captains, love, and hardship are common themes. Ancient melodies were adapted in shoreside venues, crossing from ship to pub to stage and occasionally back again. The songs of the sailors were the songs of people in harbor towns and cities, and represent a trove of primary resources about material, social, and economic culture over several centuries.

These songs have been mined by commercial composers around the world for all types of songs, overtures, tone poems, and soundtracks. These include Sir Henry Wood's "Fantasia on British Sea Songs," Charles Villiers Stanford's "Songs of the Sea," and Ralph Vaughn William's "Norfolk Rhapsodies" and "Sea Symphony." A lively, and perhaps bawdy, sailor's tune has been known to morph into a dark haunting dirge, with an airy Irish flute and stormy landscape, behind opening or closing movie credits. In turn, many classical pieces have been created to evoke the waves, storms, and the motion of sailing. After decades of popularity, Richard Wagner's "Ride of the Valkyries," Richard Rogers's "Victory at Sea," and Claude Debussey's "La Mer" are culturally valuable as emotive tools, or sources of inspiration. If we add in the Beach Boys, Jimmy Buffett, Stan Rogers, and Gordon Lightfoot, sea songs roll on.

Primary Research

There is great reward for researchers looking into the origins and stories behind the established repertoire of tunes. Advances in global communication technology have created fresh avenues and topics for research. Curiously, despite the explosion of available information, there hasn't been a sea change in our knowledge of sea songs. Most filtered up the old fashioned way, through academia and the folk process, many years ago, retaining their distinguishable inflection and energy along the way.

This is not to say that new material is not waiting to be found. On the cusp of the electronic age, an old fashioned in-the-stacks discovery unearthed a wealth of Great Lakes songs. University of Michigan literature professor Ivan Walton had a radio show and recorded regional folk music on tape. During the summer he traveled, recording and taking notes. His tenacity captured thousands of oral histories and recordings, attracted sponsors, and is preserved in the Bentley Historical Library.

Dormant for decades, Walton's work found new life in the hands of historians Joe Grimm and Lee Murdock. When the collection came to the attention of Grimm, he ran down its pedigree. Walton began his career in the 1920s, and retired in 1963. Most of the collecting was completed by 1952. By that time the sailing era was several decades gone, although the last working schooner on the lakes still existed as a museum in Detroit— rotting as it sat, and gone soon afterward. At some point Walton was convinced that his collection needed to become a book. Friends brought him together with Detroit artist Loudon Wilson to provide sketches. Wilson, a professional illustrator, employed photographs, oral histories, etchings, and antique store finds to research rigging, loading, lounging—whatever sailors did. The pen and ink illustrations are both technically correct and beautifully presented.

Figure 11.1 In the days of vinyl media, Folkways Records was among several niche public history organizations distributing sea songs and tavern ballads. From the author's collection.

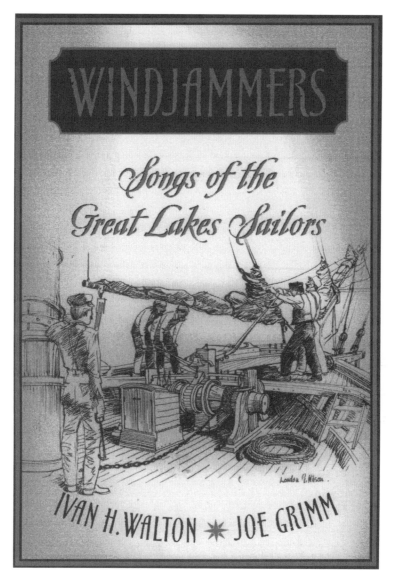

Figure 11.2 Journalist Joe Grimm brought Ivan Walton's collection of Great Lakes sea songs out of the archives, with the help of Wayne State University Press. Lee Murdock brought many of these tunes to life on a companion recording. Image from the author's collection.

Walton's book never materialized, but most of the elements were retained in the Bentley collection. Grimm convinced Wayne State University Press of their value, and they agreed to publish Joe's interpretation of Ivan's and Loudon's presumed intent. The result is "Windjammers: Songs of the Great Lakes Sailors." Grimm, a journalist by trade, beautifully melds Walton's history, Wilson's illustrations, and modern interpretation. As Walton did Wilson, so Grimm drew Murdock into collaboration; Lee, who was familiar with the Walton manuscripts, created the musical interpretation—lyrics and notation—and advised along the way. The book included a compact disc media version of many of Walton's live recordings. Lee followed up by creating modern versions of some newly revealed lyrics—interspersed with the historic Walton recordings—which he released as "Lake Rhymes, Folk Songs of the Great Lakes Region."

This wonderful melding of two generations of talent and dedication brought long overdue attention to an archival gem, and generated several publications and opportunities for public engagement. It took a century, but as a case study serves to illustrate the interpretive opportunities available to researchers who find music a fascinating arena for source material.

In the Gallery

To historians, the scratchy recording of an octogenarian, pulled from a distant vault, singing a shanty never heard before can "make your hearts' delight," quoting an Ivan Walton recording. But what is the best way to use this piece for interpretation?

Good audio elements enhance any gallery, effectively (and efficiently) putting visitors in the moment; a scratchy recording of an octogenarian singing a shanty might be just the touch your exhibit needs, either as background ambiance or a selective feature accompanying an artifact or story panel. All museum visitors have memories of audio experiences that made an exhibit special, although sometimes the best soundtrack is the one that is hardly noticed, quietly complementing the whole.

Unfortunately, many museum visitors also have memories of audio experiences that proved bothersome: too loud, too much, inappropriate, distracting, boring, or broken. If you asked some museum employees, they might add incessant, nagging, or sounds-they-hear-in-their-sleep.

There is no formula for the proper mix of sounds in a gallery. Acoustical opportunities and challenges are dictated by many things—the shape of the room, makeup and texture of the walls and floor surfaces, ceiling height and composition, HVAC, competing noises in the same space or filtering in from other galleries, speaker type and direction, nature and intensity of the sounds. Wall insulation is an important factor for installations featuring subbase effects, isolating it from other spaces. If loud sounds are used for effect, guests should be warned as they enter the gallery.

A simple formula for various uses of gallery audio might define three primary purposes: aural, authentic, and authoritative. Aural is intended to establish a mood, a time, or a place. Authentic touches the past unadulterated. Authoritative melds various media to create entertaining and instructional elements.

Aural

Purpose: to provide the "background music" of life—enjoyable, familiar, provocative—and quietly enhance an exhibition or program. It can be provided passively through electronic media. Aural can include many musical styles, including shanties, tone poems and historic soundtracks, musical theater and new music. Sound effects—waves, wharfs, wind, seagulls, creaking ships timbers—are opportunities to align with patrons' expectations, or subliminally introduce other elements—rhythm, mood, nature indoors, and so on.

Authentic

Purpose: the presentation of simple, unadulterated film tracks or audio presentations that are offered for pure perspective. They can be oral histories, radio broadcasts, recorded events, and other historic audio material, the whistle sounds from a particular factory or steamship, for instance. For greatest impact, authentic sounds are tied to a specific space or story: they define a person or event in words or sounds. Authentic noises can be used aurally, introducing visitors to a gallery, or be included as elements of an authoritative gallery narrative.

Authoritative

Purpose: to actively combine as many audio elements as appropriate to drive an instructive narrative. This might include a professionally produced film, a stage presentation, or a respected balladeer. Material of this nature is most often found in gallery videos, audio tours, auditorium presentations, and interactive electronics. Authentic and aural elements can be wedded to a script that entertains and teaches.

All three of these formats provide historical and sensual information on a number of levels. The exact formula for combining them is fluid, based on the space and technology employed. If your space includes private gallery phones or stationary listening stations, you can leverage as many audio assets as seem appropriate; sound bleed, or overlap, is not an issue. Directional speakers can help contain sounds to specific areas within a gallery. However tempting it may be, avoid placing too many audio elements in close proximity, particularly if overlapping cannot be avoided. Such situations seldom enhance the interpretive experience for guests.

In the Field

Arguably the most effective way to experience sea songs and nautical music is in live performance. Symphonic or band concerts, staged plays and musicals, folk music, and reenactment presentations can all capture an audience's imagination and make the American maritime experience come alive. Museums and historic venues regularly schedule this type of event, offering unique opportunities for visitor interaction. Some institutions include musicians and shantymen as part of their primary interpretation. Each region of North America has a community of people who specialize in local stories and songs.

The Interpreter's Perspective

This author confesses that he has been enjoying shanties and sea tunes for over thirty years, however singing is not my livelihood. To gain better perspective I interviewed Lee and Joann Murdock for this volume. Lee has made his living, since 1980, writing and performing songs about the Great Lakes region. Joann manages a number of acoustic music artists.

Figure 11.3 Lee Murdock generally performs as a solo balladeer, leveraging his distinctive voice, creative musicianship, and engaging storytelling to capture audiences. Photograph from the author's collection.

In the first few decades of the twentieth century, several books were published about or including sailors' songs. They included "Songs of Sea and Labor" by F. T. Bullen and W. F. Arnold in 1914, Joanna C. Concord's "Roll and Go, Songs of American Sailormen" in 1924," and "Sea Songs and Shanties" by Captain Whall in 1927. A few tunes filtered up into anthologies, but it was the folk revival of the 1950s and 1960s that brought shanties and ballads to the public eye, sung by the likes of Pete Seeger, Ewan MacColl, and Stan Hugill.

Lee grew up near Chicago, home to a lively folk scene, and understood the "need to differentiate yourself from other folk singers . . . the need to do different material." Folk music of the Great Lakes was a perfect niche, and it became his signature, starting in 1986 when he won an *Odyssey in the Schools* grant in Philadelphia. Since then he has kept traditional songs alive, and has written hundreds of new tunes about the ships, sailors,

Figure 11.4 As a historian, Lee Murdock is included in conference panels and focus groups. Here he takes part in a discussion of the *Lady Elgin* disaster with researchers Sharon Cook, Valerie Van Heest, and Brendon Baillod. Photograph from the author's collection.

towns, and storms of the Inland Seas. Joann commented, "Stories are the thing. If you can just get people involved in the stories."

Joann, a graphic artist and photographer, handles much of the booking and marketing for the business. Together they've worked with museums, schools, libraries, historical organizations, public events, and concert organizers. Lee points out that this puts people in his occupation— musicians, storytellers, craftsmen—in the unique position of liaison between these many cultural institutions. Together, Joann and Lee know most of the leaders and resources in the Great Lakes maritime sphere. They have seen what works, what doesn't work, and where opportunities exist.

So you want to be a folk singer? Go for it.

- As an interpretive channel, live music offers a variety of opportunities for both the musician and the venue. Audience satisfaction and performer satisfaction are closely tied. If you enjoy performing, go make people happy. If your museum or event is considering enhancements to a maritime exhibit or programming, hire a

Figure 11.5 Flexibility is essential for success as a performer of regionally unique folk music. Here Lee Murdock performs at Fayette, Michigan, formerly a booming iron smelting town turned ghost town. Today it is a state park. Photograph courtesy of Joann and Lee Murdock.

good shanteyman. (Note to musicians: Performing without an invitation at any venue is not recommended, if you want to get hired later.)

- This is a calling that can be a blast, but being an independent musician means you are your own business. The artistic part—researching and writing, performing and teaching—is tremendously rewarding. The other half—the business part—is equally important, but nowhere near as much fun: marketing, publicity, travel arrangements, equipment maintenance and depreciation, and accounting.

- Publicity is the biggest part of the job. Traditional and social media are both necessary. Take advantage of electronic postings (boatnerd.com), blogs, Facebook, and whatever comes along in the next few year. Person-to-person relationships are essential for getting the word out. As with politics, local media can be powerful.

- Persistence pays. There are doors and gatekeepers at institutions large and small, but once you get past them opportunities abound.

- Get as many experiences as possible; it's hard to write about sailing if you haven't been on a boat.

What works?

- Create an event—memorial, anniversary, accomplishment. Create a focus for publicity, and make it an annual "thing." The Murdocks created their first event around Chicago's "Christmas Tree Ship," the schooner *Rouse Simmons*, which brought freshly cut Christmas trees to the Chicago docks for many years, before being lost on Lake Michigan. This popular family-friendly holiday program is staged annually in Illinois, Michigan, Ohio, and Wisconsin. For nearly a decade, Lee has performed at the Lost Mariners Remembrance on November 10 at the Dossin Great Lakes Museum in Detroit. He is a regular presenter at dive shows, history gatherings, yacht club events, and music festivals throughout the Midwest.
- Mix it up—Do what you can to get a diverse conversation going. Lee asked, "What do you do to get people in the door and mixing them up?" Performance art draws divers, techies, folklorists, musicians, writers, historians, sailors, artists, and archaeologists. "It is happening organically in local historical organizations and gatherings, county fairs. Cross pollinating, as it were."
- Teachers are highly receptive to live performance and music in an educational environment. Grants for in-school programming have been steadily declining, but Lee and Joann agree that partnerships with museums and teachers can be hugely rewarding.
- Train your audience. There's a fine line between traditional (an annual event that people enjoy) and predictable (an annual event that people ignore). Be consistent, be convenient, and be creative. Let them anticipate a great event—anticipation being a large part of the fun.

Note

1. Stan Hugill, ed., *Shanties from the Seven Seas: Shipboard Work-Songs and Songs Used as Work-Songs from the Great Days of Sail* (London: Routledge & Kegan Paul, 1984 [2nd ed.]), 2–6.

CHAPTER 12

DIFFICULT MARITIME TOPICS

JOEL STONE

THERE HAS BEEN an insightful dialog among museum professionals, over recent decades, about presenting tough topics in public spaces. Exhibitions and interpretations show an increased willingness or incentive to approach difficult histories, and elevate their voice in the social chorus. "Such claims to social agency propels museums and historical sites into a wider and more urgent educational role of advocating for social justice," says Julia Rose in *Interpreting Difficult History at Museums and Historic Sites*.[1] This increased responsibility offers opportunities, but with risk. An open—even aggressive—approach has the benefit of altering preconceived notions and introducing historical mindsets to today's thinkers. It can also alienate or even frighten some visitors.

There is no shortage of difficult topics: race relations, class or ethnic intolerance, genocide, crime, poverty, brutality, sexism, religious absolutism, political imperialism, social responsibility, slavery, gangs, smuggling, drug and human trafficking. There is also no shortage of ways in which to approach difficult topics, among them truth, humor, shock, inclusion, immersion, media framing, social advocacy, and oral history or oral tradition.

Unfortunately, as Erica Lehrer and Cynthia E. Milton point out in the introduction to *Curating Difficult Knowledge*, "in an age saturated with media images of human suffering and ever-democratizing technologies for their dissemination, simply making people face the horrors humans are capable of perpetrating seems to have lost some of its galvanizing force."[2] Public history professionals must understand this overload as they increasingly explore empathy and cross-cultural dialog "to recognize multiple perspectives, or to catalyze action." As diverse voices are drawn into the museum "safe space," there must be a simultaneous heightening of awareness among curators and presenters, not only of the value of each perspective, but of our audience's capacity for absorbing and processing the ever-broader spectrum. Amping up message volume can be counterproductive. As it is possible to lose your guests to a boring exhibit or presentation, it is equally simple to drive them away with overstimulation or excessive pedantry.

There are ways to interpret without overwhelming or bludgeoning. As exemplified by the Jim Crow Museum, the basic act of displaying select artifacts, with limited interpretation, can have a tremendous impact. In the same vein, using dialog from documents or oral histories—not a didactic voice, but that of the historic participants—allows the curator to send clear messages that are immediately authentic and, when necessary, poignant.

An important challenge of any historic interpretation is developing within your guests a historic mindset, allowing them to understand the characters and situations they are encountering apart (or as apart as possible) from modern mores and expectations. Presentations can get derailed when they stridently decry atrocities of the past with the admonishing voice of the present. While the atrocities might indeed be vile, it is not fair to our ancestors or guests to represent them without context. Leaving such bias aside, difficult stories are easier to tell, and lose little of their impact.

It is up to individual curators or interpretive teams to decide what is right for their situation, whether it's an installation, topical publication, live presentation, panel discussion, conservation initiative, or a myriad of other options. What is the message, and what information is vital to that message? Is the narrative better developed by a native or an outsider—that is, intimate passion or neutral analysis? What best serves your audience?

In maritime interpretation, the most sensitive topics tend to be the most popular as well as the most polarizing. They can include military actions, shipwrecks, piracy, whaling, slavery, and immigration.

Military Actions

Military actions are detailed throughout history. Following each event, voluminous records and accounts are continually analyzed in seminars and monographs. In the last century, interpretation was focused on tactics and technology. Since the mass media era began, the vision has included an increasingly personal side of war. Stories that hadn't been told for years finally emerge, lending subtle shading to the stark black and white of official records.

As in war, there are landmines waiting in military event commemoration. Stories of individual soldiers can be hugely personal, especially if the family is still active in the retelling. Occasionally, when reliable research confronts family lore it can offer difficult but teachable moments. The solid data may dispute the lore, but both are part of the historic record. How often have we encountered an erroneous story, oft repeated, that becomes fact—or lore? It can be difficult to set the record straight, but the lore often becomes as historically important as the truth. Think George Washington and the apple tree. Both can be leveraged to enhance interpretation.

This topic is discussed in modest depth in the next chapter. For more information about the fighting maritime and its commemoration, refer to *Interpreting Naval History* by Dr. Ben Hruska, part of the AASLH Interpreting History Series published by Rowman & Littlefield.

Shipwrecks

Shipwrecks are perhaps the most tragic of sea disasters. Unrelated to the vagaries of man, politics, and engineering, wrecks are most often pure Nature at work. Attributed to the will of gods or physical forces, Nature—storms and tides in concert with expansive seas and leeward shallows—sent millions of humans to their deaths. Some of those travelers were at war. Some carried hopes for a new life. Some bore tons of gold bullion. Some were on vacation. Some were captives. A majority were just doing their job. Sometimes, rescuers were involved, successful or not; sometimes vessels simply disappeared. Inevitably owners, insurance agents, lawyers, courts, survivors, and salvagers add to the record. Balladeers and poets reinterpret notable shipwrecks, and the media relates notable anniversaries.

When interpreting shipwrecks it is most important to respect the memory of the vessel and the lives lost. Mariners admit that the ships they work on display traits, perhaps personalities. Some say they have souls.

In shipboard emergencies, sailors might give everything to save their mates, or perhaps perform terrible momentary acts of cowardice. Interpreters who disparage a ship or its crew should proceed cautiously. Like military actions, shipwrecks are often reported from numerous perspectives that don't always agree. The disparities can be an interesting interpretive tool, prompting visitors to seek and analyze facts in search of the truth.

Piracy

Interpretations of piracy have varied over time, and today can vary depending on the audience and period addressed. Piracy is found in maritime histories around the world on both saltwater and fresh water. While the term generally evokes images of rogues from the eighteenth century, pirates are still active and, at this writing, represent one of the most dangerous aspects of sailing in many parts of the world.

Historically, privately owned vessels commanded by aggressive and opportunistic sailors were sanctioned by governments to protect that government's global interests. Depending on who wrote your history, these mariners were pirates or heroes. Francis Drake was a pirate to Spaniards and a hero to Englishmen. In the early twenty-first century, piracy has proven profitable in countries like Somalia, Nigeria, and Malaysia, and as close to home as Nicaragua.

In North America, the romantic notion of a pirate has been cultivated through literature, film, and amusement park rides. The men known as cavaliers, buccaneers, swashbucklers, and freebooters were often sailors discharged from national navies between wars. Opportunism provided employment. Discipline, victuals, and remuneration were better than in naval or commercial positions, and depended on brutal success.

Interpreting thievery and murder at sea, debauchery and crime ashore is both exciting and worthy of caution. Similar to whaling, piracy is gory and cruel. Local interpretation should be exciting, and—truth being stranger than fiction—can generally be effective by sticking to the facts. Individual institutions and interpreters must decide how much of the really nasty history—prostitution, venereal disease, mass execution—they wish to include.

Of course, for the younger set piracy can be an *entre pônt* for capturing imaginations. Dress up activities, walking the plank, fencing maneuvers, or gun drills are options for group activities, but it should be tactfully explained that there were deadly consequences for everything except the dressing up.

Whaling

Whaling is an ancient industry that peaked in the nineteenth century and is still practiced in a few cultures. Shifts in American perceptions of whaling and the near annihilation of several species prompted a general reversal in the North American approach to both the animal and interpretation of the business. This recent shift in attitudes has had a significant influence on interpretation.

American whaling blossomed from a cottage industry in the mid-1600s to a refined and profitable maritime niche a century later. By the time of the American Civil War, whalers of the US fleet ruled the worldwide market. In 1857, there were 329 vessels sailing out of New Bedford alone—one of many ports—roaming the globe to secure valuable oil, spermaceti, and meat. For decades, whale oil lamps were America's most efficient illumination.

Tools of the industry, from the stout whaling ships to blubber hooks and trypots, tell tales of a maritime lifestyle experienced by tens of thousands of sailors. It was a tough life; the voyages could be three or four years long, the work more dangerous and dirty than most sailors experienced (a poor benchmark), and pay dependent upon a successful catch. However, whaling became a North American heritage focal point for ports in the Northeast, West Coast, and Hawaii, and "part of the story" in numerous other seaside communities.

Americans abandoned the business as the worldwide fishery collapsed in the early twentieth century. Electricity and petroleum products replaced whale oil as a fuel. Nations that relied on the meat for food continued to invest in whaling. During the latter part of the century, the environmental movement put a public spotlight on the near extinction of certain whale species.

With international stewardship, the worldwide whale population has rebounded. Today, technology has improved efficiency, and those nations still operating whaling ships are sensitive to maintaining sustainable populations. However, divergent cultural attitudes between people in many western nations and the whaling countries of Japan, Norway, and Iceland should be considered when interpreting this subject.

For further insight be sure to read Erik Ingmundson's interpretation of the American whaleship *Charles W. Morgan* earlier in this volume.

Slavery

Apart from the Underground Railroad, discussed in the next chapter, slavery is an important narrative within the maritime world. Certainly, the triangle trade, from Europe to Africa and on to the Americas, stands today as a difficult chapter in maritime commerce. So too are the slave traditions among indigenous populations. Slavery was equally a term applicable to sailors. Impressment of sailors at sea or ashore, by various navies, is a perfect example of the commodity nature of able-bodied seamen, but seldom is Jack Tar described as a slave.

For most of a sailor's life, a strict hierarchy dictated his activities, his comfort, food, and safety. There was little recourse for the seaman; to complain could mean physical retribution, and refusing an order meant death. In the words of labor historian Bruce Nelson, sailors "entered the twentieth century bearing the burden of an archaic, semi-feudal tradition of the sea and a code of laws that perpetuated [their] bondage."[3] Legislation in the United States democratized the on-board relationships between sailors and officers between 1915 and 1920, and established health and safety standards.

However, even today the polyglot population employed at sea lives on the hairy edge of slavery, at the mercy of cost-cutting employers, modern-day pirates, and nature. A captivating examination of their plight is captured in Rose George's *Ninety Percent of Everything* cited earlier in this book. For more on African American slavery see *Interpreting Slavery at Museums and Historic Sites*, edited by Kristin L. Gallas and James DeWolf Perry.

Immigration

Immigration is everyone's story. We are all immigrants, and prior to the 1950s nearly every immigrant to North American came by watercraft. Some took boats deep into the interior before getting on a trail, train, or coach. It is a massive story and not always easy to tell. Political opinion about immigration in the United States has been historically polarizing.

For historians and curators, there is an easy empathy that makes immigrant tales popular. Government records, now available electronically, have made genealogical research far more efficient. Within the public history realm, archival documents allow a curator, designer, educator, or interpreter to tell an authentic story without generating new content.

This should be easy, yet within the story of the *Amistad* is both hope and tragedy. Within the story of the Mariel boatlift is hope and tragedy. So, too, in the *Titanic*'s tale, and those currently coming from the eastern Mediterranean. For millions of new Americans, there was a seaborne adventure that was remembered for life—for better or worse—and became an almost-universal immigrant experience.

It should not be forgotten that some migrant groups, once in North America, made their living from the water. As mentioned earlier, early Anglo immigrants cornered the whaling trade. Gallic and Scandinavian arrivals became invested in fishing and furs. Greeks in Florida created a thriving trade in sponge harvesting, as did Acadians in the Louisiana shrimp business.

Notes

1. Julia Rose, *Interpreting Difficult History at Museums and Historic Sites* (Lanham, MD: Rowman and Littlefield, 2016), 8.

2. Erica Lehrer and Cynthia E. Milton, eds., *Curating Difficult Knowledge: Violent Pasts in Public Places* (London: Palgrave Macmillan, 2011), 1.

3. Bruce Nelson, *Workers on the Waterfront* (Urbana: University of Illinois Press, 1988), 12.

CHAPTER 13

THE "OTHER" ASPECTS OF MARITIME HISTORIES

Joel Stone

T HIS VOLUME has limited itself to seven case studies and a few observational chapters. However, within the history of waterborne transportation there are a number of other interpretive topics that must be explored, albeit in less depth. These include: military history and maritime remembrance; Native American maritime cultures; the role of maritime in the Underground Railroad story; various North American ethnic immigrant groups and their relationship with the water; maritime topics that might be difficult to interpret for various reasons; and elements of maritime history that are seldom linked to boats or ships.

These various histories are no less important than those discussed in the case studies. When it comes to military history, most maritime museums include some element of naval warfare. The stories tend to be local. Similarly, the Native American relationship with the water is ancient, and regional. The story of migrants—be they Vikings, Delaware, enslaved or indentured people seeking freedom, or those debarking at Ellis Island— are stories that inevitably involve boats. We encounter sensitive topics—they involve violence, death, and tragedy.

Military History

Naval history commands the highest profile in maritime history and maritime museums. From earliest times, boats were built and manned to aggressively protect commerce. Three thousand years ago, Phoenicians developed some of the earliest ships designed specifically for war. Few major world powers have maintained their dominance without maritime supremacy.

Military maritime history is broad. It includes important political forces, renowned admirals, legendary battles, famous ships, tactical geniuses, and unaccountable cruelties and tragedies. It also addresses little-known encounters prompted by misunderstood diplomacy, accidental victories caused by flukes of wind or tide, and compassionate prologues about enemies saving enemies.

Interpretation is exponentially broader. Any of these scenarios could involve a discussion of the ships, weaponry, strategies, timelines, casualties, repercussions, and overall impact on the larger conflict. As a view-from-the-deck presentation involves people, any exhibition or presentation might include descriptions of the captains and crews, their duties, living conditions, food, training, drills, duties, rules, loves, arts, and hobbies.

Most of the maritime institutions in North America that interpret naval history treat the topic geographically. Exhibits focus on local men who served, vessels built in local shipyards, and battles fought in local waters. The proximity to landmarks or the vessels themselves offer powerful opportunity to connect with guests.

Naval history is thoroughly chronicled and artifact rich. Government correspondence, logs, letters, ledgers, manifests, agency and newspaper reports, vendor and supplier records, photographs, plans and diagrams are all available from North America's early colonial period through today. Public and private institutions have been collecting material culture for decades, and have rich repositories of artifacts, images, documents, and ephemera to enhance an exhibit story. The US Navy and US Coast Guard both have excellent collections, as do museums, museum ships, universities, lighthouses, and libraries.

This topic is covered in detail in *Interpreting Maritime Military History* by Dr. Ben Hruska, part of the AASLH Interpreting History Series published by Rowman & Littlefield.

Maritime Remembrance

As a medium for transportation, water can be tranquil or brutal. The good days produce sunsets and rainbows. The bad days can be awe-filled and fatal. Whether in war or peace, sailors, passengers, fortunes, and dreams have been lost at sea. Those left behind mourn.

For millennia, survivors have expressed their grief publicly on monuments, plaques, parks, and headstones, as well as in songs, poems, and artifacts, so that relatives and friends "not be lost to the knowledge of men." The records of the landscape, the literature, and remembrance traditions tell a rich and ongoing tale.

Commemorations take a number of forms. Anniversaries are marked with gatherings and reflection, often accompanied by historical interpretation and special presentations. The laying of wreaths is a common component, as is the solemn ringing of bells and firing of cannons. Where a memorial site is accessible by water, flotillas of boats participate in the ancient custom of spreading flowers on the waves.

Memorial events don't have to be funereal, but should be respectful. A perfect example is the Lost Mariners Remembrance program held annually at the Dossin Great Lakes Museum in Detroit. The day before Veterans Day, November 10, coincidently marks the day that the famed SS *Edmund Fitzgerald* sank in a Lake Superior storm. The two-hour event starts with a Lantern Ceremony around one of the Fitzgerald's anchors outside the museum. A lantern is lit for each crewman, and a friend or family member will proffer a short memory or prayer. Guests then move into the museum for a musical presentation of Great Lakes ballads.

A Wreath Ceremony follows, with bagpipers leading an honor guard, composed of officers from branches of military and merchant marine, who accompany the wreath to the riverside. A flotilla of vessels from US and Canadian sea services passes in review. A US Coast Guard patrol boat takes the wreath to the middle of the Detroit River. At 7:10 p.m. (1910 EST), the time the Fitzgerald sank, the flowers are committed to the river. A helicopter illuminates the floating wreath with spotlights and flares, and passing commercial ships sound salutes. Buglers play Taps and Last Post. Guests are offered the opportunity to drop roses in the river to commemorate their own family and friends.

Participants return inside for a presentation about the year's featured craft or event—a vessel disaster or notable storm likely tied to an anniversary. The speaker's historical perspective is followed by a nondenominational benediction, and performance of Gordon Lightfoot's "Wreck of the Edmund Fitzgerald," accompanied by the ringing of a large steamboat bell, tolling for all lost mariners. The entire program takes about two hours, and has been sold out for many years. Perhaps the most unique aspect of this program is the volunteer, multinational participation of military and police units at all levels from both the United States and Canada, including the International Shipmasters Association, the Great Lake Maritime Institute, and the port authorities of both Detroit and Windsor, Ontario. Funding comes largely from the independent US Lake Carriers' Association and the Canadian Shipowners Association. It is the only such international ceremony in the country.

I cite this example because it is familiar to me, and includes many of the most common elements of commemorative ceremonies. These methods, and variations of them, are used around the world to remember tragedies at sea. For more information about maritime remembrance, refer to *Interpreting Naval History* by Dr. Ben Hruska, part of the AASLH Interpreting History Series published by Rowman & Littlefield.

Native American Maritime

When imagining native cultures, we don't necessarily equate them with vast maritime trade networks, refined vessel design, and skilled seamanship. Yet in North America and the South Pacific, indigenous people have relied on boats and rafts in commerce for millennia. It's an important story which has only gradually emerged in the Native American narrative. The problem—there's not a lot to work with.

Historian Howard Chappelle, in his treatise on native craft construction, notes that the nature of the bark, reed, and skin boats do not lend themselves to long-term preservation. Besides dugout craft preserved in bogs, researchers have recorded descriptions beginning in 1535, as well as traditional practices studied and revived in the last century.[1]

Physical evidence in the forms of cities and villages, burial mounds, mines, petroglyphs, shell middens, and hunting sites confirm man's early affinity to the water for both sustenance and transportation. Oral traditions are also rich with allusions to people interacting with maritime environments and deities. By the time Europeans arrived, marine commerce was so developed as to reflect regional and tribal variations in design and use.

Participation in the early maritime was in direct relation to proximity to water. Desert people were not sailors; however there is evidence that Paleolithic people in northern Mexico acquired copper mined on the northern Great Lakes, a trade estimated to be five thousand years old. The copper ore likely spent time in a canoe, the super cargo carrier of mid-continental rivers and lakes. Along every coast, native sailors used boats to communicate, to transport their harvest—fish, grain, furs, lumber—and to facilitate military actions.

Geography dictated vessel type and build. Arctic umiaks and kayaks were of skin and wood or bone lathe, and canoes of the upper Midwest and East coast were of bark and wood lathe. In the South Pacific, Gulf of Mexico, and lower Mississippi waters, dugout canoes were viable. While characteristics of the boat were different, the intent of the builders was usually the same—efficiency and survival. A twelve-meter birch bark canoe can carry four tons of furs, supplies, or warriors at a speed of 3.5 to 5 miles per hour, covering fifty to seventy miles in a day.

Interpretation, like boat design, is regional. Each tribe or clan has particular cultural traditions related to maritime skill, technologies, and legends—they are often related, but the dissimilarities are important. Tribal museums, archives, and intertribal events are good starting points for inspiration and direction.

While the art of bark canoe building has nearly disappeared, even among native practitioners, there are still craftsmen available to do workshops and lectures. Fort William Historical Park, in Thunder Bay, Ontario, has a bark canoe shed in constant production and offers rides to visitors. Other museums have sponsored on-site construction of canoes and kayaks, among them the Abbe Museum in Maine, the Canadian Canoe Museum in Ontario, Apalachicola Maritime Museum, Lake Champlain Maritime Museum, and the Columbia River Maritime Museum.

Further information about interpreting Native American history can be found in *Interpreting Native American History and Culture at Museums and Historic Sites* by Raney Bench, part of the AASLH Interpreting History Series published by Rowman & Littlefield.

Underground Railroad Afloat

It is well known that nearly every African brought to North America as a slave came in a sailing ship. What is not always considered is that most unfree persons traveling north to escape slavery traveled by boat somewhere in their journey. No matter their route, mighty rivers presented obstacles, and people traveling undercover eschewed bridges. Sometimes they swam, if they had that skill, or were ferried in rowboats and canoes. However, a significant number availed themselves of commercial steamboats and sailing craft in their quest for freedom.

Along the Atlantic Coast, the opportunities were great. Regular packet vessels, either sail or steam, carried black servants accompanying masters and traveling freedmen, and were served by a large contingent of black sailors. Servants were known to escape when in northern ports, freedmen were found with forged or borrowed papers, and black sailors proved potent allies to runaways. There are many credible stories of slaves crating themselves as cargo and shipping themselves north. Additionally, several American ships were owned by northern investors whose religious affiliations made them sympathetic to abolitionist causes.

The stories of Henry Brown, Robert Smalls—who commandeered an armed Confederate Navy ship—Harriet Jacobs, and William and Ellen Craft are all tales of bravery and the Underground maritime.

Further inland the opportunities were greater. In the 1840s–1850s, railroads were just beginning to make inroads to the continent, generally in an east-west direction. Going south-to-north depended on the Mississippi, Ohio, and Missouri rivers and their many tributaries—all served by established and efficient steamboats, and all leading toward Canada. It was common in river towns, from Louisiana to Minnesota, to see Negroes working as wharf laborers and deckhands, providing potential cover, assistance, and even employment for transient blacks.

On the northern lakes, steamboats carried thousands of people to freedom in Canada. Most were ferried from places along the St. Lawrence, Niagara, Detroit, and St. Clair rivers, into Canada West (today Ontario); Ogdensburg, Buffalo, Detroit, and Port Huron were funnels for freedom seekers. Opportunities were also available at Chicago, Kenosha, and Milwaukee to ship eastward toward Goderich or Windsor. Travelers arriving at Erie, Cleveland, Sandusky, or Toledo could board steamships for Detroit; when necessary, there would be a stop at Malden (today Amherstburg) to take on Canadian firewood. Debarking passengers were often met by local citizens, there to assist with the transition to a new life beyond slavery.

Every region except the West Coast has a rich history with the Underground Railroad. Legend and fact get blurred, and historians debate. Quilts with codes—are they real? Secret signals—did that happen? Possibly, but on an informal basis; there wasn't a nationwide runaway slave code.

White abolitionists ran the railroad, right? Not usually. Much of the organizational leadership and boots on the ground were black. The command structure was black and white. Support—fiscal and physical, political and private—came from whites and blacks. The majority who made the system work were black.

Perhaps the greatest interpretive mistake is misunderstanding the animosity escaping slaves faced in northern states. Reaching the states of Ohio or Michigan did not ensure freedom, particularly after enactment of the 1850 Fugitive Slave Law; Canada was the only real safe haven. The majority of northerners either supported the South's right to have slaves, or didn't have time to worry about it. Those of the nativist persuasion, members of the American Party and many Democrats, wanted blacks to remain in the south, or be resettled in Africa. Newly settled immigrants—the primary target of nativists—were busting sod, building businesses, and trying to establish themselves in new homes.

We know of thousands of reported "stations" on Underground Railroad routes, and thousands more well outside of established routes. Each of these potential stops has a story worth telling, even if it's not verifiable. Is this a family legend passed down through generations, reflecting a pride in participation—even if the evidence is negligible? How many station keepers only served once, by choice (spiritual or political activism) or opportunity (no one ever knocked again)?

Graphic interpretation is hampered by the clandestine nature of the Underground Railroad. For travelers, the brief experience—a few weeks out of a lifetime—left few remaining artifacts. The Underground Railroad is much like the illegal trade in alcohol during US Prohibition in the 1920s: from an organizational standpoint, communications were guarded, records nonexistent, and tangible evidence minimal. This can be a real challenge for historians or curators.

Despite the paucity of interpretive "bling," there are very creative and successful ways to bring the Underground Railroad into your museum and historic venues. Further information about interpreting Underground Railroad history can be found in *Interpreting African American History and Culture at Museums and Historic Sites* by Max van Balgooy, and in *Interpreting Slavery at Museums and Historic Sites*, edited by Kristin L. Gallas and James DeWolf Perry. Both books are part of the AASLH Interpreting History Series published by Rowman & Littlefield.

Cruise Ships, Scuba, and Surfing

In 2014 the American cruise ship market carried fourteen million people and generated over $21 billion.[2] It would be hard to deny that this is a significant part of our maritime heritage. But how do cruise ships, sailing, fishing, scuba diving, or surfing fit into that heritage picture? If we recall the parameters set forth in the introductory chapter, *maritime* involves cultures on land and at sea whose viability depends upon ships or shoreside commerce. There is no question that surfing is its own culture, but beyond that its two million American practitioners depend on waves for their tiny "ships," and annually support a multibillion dollar shoreside industry.

Recreational boating, from a historical standpoint, was described beautifully by John Summers in chapter 10. Yet today—tomorrow's history—it remains a huge, multisegmented aspect of our economy. In 2013 the National Marine Manufacturers Association (NMMA) stated that recreational boating in the United States represented an annual economic value of $121.5 billion and supported almost a million induced, direct, and indirect American jobs each year. Better yet, almost all of the boats sold in the United States—$16.4 billion—are built in the United States.[3] Scuba diving in 2014 generated over $500 million and employed twelve thousand people; 40 percent of those resources came from new divers, a growing demographic.[4] From a practical standpoint, the recreational maritime industries have been one of the most productive segments of American businesses, outside the governmental sphere. From deck-level, serious recreational sailors have an equally close relationship with navigation, tides, safety, and boat handling as the best commercial deckhands.

Despite its long history, the recreational maritime is in decline. A 1998 NMMA survey listed 16.8 million noncommercial, registered watercraft. By 2010 that number had fallen to 12.5 million, a 26 percent reduction. Arguably, the Great Recession affected those numbers, but the first part of that twelve-year period was one of spending excess;

once the purchase is made, owners tend to maintain registrations as long as they still own the boat.[5]

This is the recreational maritime's greatest advantage within public history. Anywhere in the nation, there is a broad spectrum of people who have some experience "messing about in boats." Those who participate in the myriad of activities have an immediate affinity to its history. Whether it is sailing songs or fishing lures, the opportunities to connect are many.

From a programming standpoint, boat shows, fishing tournaments, outboard motor swaps, and canoe races continue to be part of local calendars. Partnerships with these organizations are essential—and generally fun! You likely won't have the resources to participate at every function, but even a moderate profile expresses support for the overall mission. From a curatorial standpoint, when developing new exhibitions, the contacts made at these events can prove invaluable for artifact generation, research material, fundraising, and programming.

There is actually a second "greatest advantage" to the recreational maritime. It is generally about fun, and beauty, and speed and daring, and relaxation and nature. That can be an easy sell in exhibition form.

Maritime in Art and Advertising

This particular niche is a wonderful scholastic reservoir, though generally overlooked. Because steamboats and packet carriers were major players in the transportation industry through 1910, their place in American art, advertising, and iconography is understood, but not widely studied. It offers great fodder for interpretation.

As the airline industry does today, so did the passenger ships appeal to elegance—speed, comfort, and affordability—starting around 1830. Shipping companies often commissioned painted portraits of their ships to be displayed in ticket offices. Vessels and companies branded the china and silver in their dining rooms; where preserved, these are invaluable interpretive tools. With the development of sophisticated printing processes, they spread the word with enticing illustrations on placards, advertisements, and billboards. One of the most widely distributed lithographs of the late 1880s was a marine scene titled "Champion and Tow," depicting a tug named *Champion* pulling schooners into the head of the Detroit River. A decade later it was illustrations of the distinctive passenger steamer *Christopher Columbus* that captivated the Columbia Exposition throngs. Shipwrecks, famous tea clippers, naval battles, and yachts were favorite topics as the twentieth century dawned.

In a broader sense, there is an American maritime art tradition dating to prehistory. As an interpretive tool, few things are more engaging than petroglyphs or woven baskets. In a narrower sense, the earliest of American towns likely sat on a river or shore, where early commerce began. Advertising in local papers often justifies the sobriquet "harbor" or "port town" with block prints of ships that can be evocative and seem completely out of context today.

Associated—but Often Ignored—Topics

There are many maritime genres that are seldom highlighted in public installations, programs, or collections. For instance, law enforcement is part of the "Prohibition Navy" or "War on Drugs" stories, but the Revenue Cutter Service is nearly lost to history.

Exhibitions on important events in marine politics are rare. Even rarer are installations about important rulings in maritime law. While these might be challenging topics to interpret, they can offer rich insight to your visitors—maritime history is not just boats and pirates.

Going forward curators and educators should consider every installation as having a potential maritime component. Cloth and clothing have strong ties to maritime, both past and present. Electronic devices, food, textbooks, furniture, building products, car parts—you name it and behind the glitzy packaging and marketing there is a ship. Maritime history is everywhere. Opportunities for interpretation are everywhere.

Notes

1. Edwin Tappan Adney and Howard Chappelle, *The Bark Canoes and Skin Boats of North America* (Washington, D.C.: Smithsonian Institution, 1964).

2. http://www.statista.com/topics/1004/cruise-industry/.

3. http://www.nmma.org/press/article/18375.

4. https://c.ymcdn.com/sites/www.dema.org/resource/resmgr/Research_Documents/Diving_Fast_Facts-2014.pdf.

5. National Marine Manufacturers Association 1998 report, http://oceanservice.noaa.gov/websites/retiredsites/natdia_pdf/14boatus.pdf; 2010 report at http://www.nmma.org/press/article/18028.

BIBLIOGRAPHY

Adams, Jonathan. "Ships and Boats as Archaeological Source Material." *World Archaeology* 32(3) (2001): 292–310.

Adney, Edwin Tappan, and Howard Chappelle, *The Bark Canoes and Skin Boats of North America.* Washington, D.C.: Smithsonian Institution, 1964.

Akin, Gainor, R. "The Morgan Floats!" *Windrose*, January 1974, 1–6. [*Windrose* is a quarterly membership newsletter published by Mystic Seaport.]

Albelli, Leonardo, Massimiliano Secci, and Pier Giorgio I. Spanu. "The Roman Conquest of Pantilleria through Recent Underwater Investigations: From Discovery to Public Outreach and Public Access to Maritime Cultural Heritage." In *ACUA Underwater Archaeology Proceedings 2014*, edited by Charles Dagneau and Karolyn Gauvin, 345–55. Germantown, MD: Advisory Council on Underwater Archaeology, 2014.

Anderson, Bern. *By Sea and By River: the Naval History of the Civil War.* New York: Alfred A. Knopf, 1962.

Anderson, Gail, ed. *Reinventing the Museum.* Lanham, MD: AltaMira Press, 2004.

Andrews, Israel D. "Communication from the Secretary of the Treasury Transmitting . . . the Report of Israel D. Andrews . . . on the Trade and Commerce of the British North American Colonies, and upon the Trade of the Great Lakes and Rivers. . . ." Washington, D.C.: Robert Armstrong, 1853.

Arenson, Sarah. "The Underwater Archaeological Park at Herod's Sunken Harbor of Sebastos (Caesaria Maritima)." *Leon Recanati Institute for Maritime Studies News* 32(2006): 14–16.

Beeker, Charles D., and Frederick H. Hanselmann. "The Wreck of the *Cara Merchant*: Investigations of Captain Kidd's Lost Ship." In *ACUA Underwater Archaeology Proceedings 2009*, edited by E. Laanela and J. Moore, 219–26. Germantown, MD: Advisory Council on Underwater Archaeology, 2009.

Bercaw-Edwards, Mary K. Interview by the author. Mystic Seaport Museum, Mystic, CT. February 4, 2016.

Boyd, Kelly, ed. *Encyclopedia of Historians and Historical Writing.* Vol. 2. London: Fitzroy Dearborn, 1999.

Broeze, Frank. *Maritime History at the Crossroads: A Critical Review of Recent Historiography.* St. John's, Newfoundland: International Maritime Economic History Association, 1995.

Brown, Sara. "Last of Her Kind, Whaleship Charles W. Morgan Has Strong Ties to the Vineyard." *Vineyard Gazette.* Last modified July 20, 2014. Accessed February 15, 2016, http://vineyardgazette.com/news/2014/06/20/last-her-kind-whaleship-charles-w-morgan -has-strong-ties-vineyard.

Burke, Peter. *What Is Cultural History?* Malden, MA: Polity, 2004.

Cangany, Catherine. *Frontier Seaport.* Chicago: University of Chicago, 2014.

Carleton, Guy. "Letter to John Graves Simcoe, 25 January 1796." In *Correspondence of Lieut. Governor John Graves Simcoe, with Allied Documents Relating to His Administration of the Government of Upper Canada*. Vol. 4, p. 181 (1923–1931). Ontario Historical Society, Toronto, ON.

Chambers, Clarke A. "The 'New' Social History, Local History, and Community Empowerment." *Minnesota History* (Spring 1984): 14–18.

Chappelle, Howard I. *History of American Sailing Ships*. New York: W.W. Norton, 1935.

Chouzenoux, Christelle. *Caractérisation et Typologie du Cimitière des Ancres*. [Characterization and Typology of the Anchor Graveyard]. M.A. thesis, Universidade Fernando Pessoa, Portugal, 2011.

Cohn, Arthur B. "Lake Champlain's Underwater Archaeological Preserve Program: Reasonable Access to Appropriate Sites." In *Submerged Cultural Resource Management: Preserving and Interpreting our Sunken Maritime Heritage*, edited by James D. Spirek and Della Scott-Ireton, 88. New York: Kluwer Academic/Plenum Press, 2003.

Conlin, David L., and Larry E. Murphy, Lake Meade National Recreation Area B-29 Management Plan: Technical Report No. 23 (Santa Fe: National Park Service Submerged Resources Center, 2006).

Conlin, David L., and Matthew A. Russell. "Site Formation Processes Once Removed: Pushing the Boundaries of Interdisciplinary Maritime Archaeology." In *ACUA Underwater Archaeology Proceedings 2009*, edited by E. Laanela and J. Moore, 83–90. Germantown, MD: Advisory Council on Underwater Archaeology, 2009.

Council of American Maritime Museums (CAAM). "Membership List." Accessed February 2016, https://councilofamericanmaritimemuseums.org/member-directory/.

Cruikshank, Jeffrey, and Chloe G. Kline. *In Peace and War: A History of the U.S. Merchant Marine Academy at Kings Point*. Hoboken, NJ: Wiley, 2008.

Dana, John Cotton. "The Gloom of the Museum." In *Reinventing the Museum*, edited by Gail Anderson, 17–33. Lanham, MD: AltaMira, 2012.

Ebert, David. "Applications of Archaeological GIS." *Canadian Journal of Archaeology* 28(2) (2004): 319–41.

Engelman, Elysa. Interview. Mystic Seaport Museum, Mystic, CT. February 3, 2016.

English Heritage. "Advisory Committee of Historic Wreck Sites Annual Report 2009." London: Department for Culture, Media and Sport, 2010. Accessed January 25, 2016, http://www.english-heritage.org.uk/publications/achws-annual-report-2009/achws-2009-10-ann-rep.pdf.

Evangelista, Joe, Steward H. Wade, Caryln Swaim, and James P. Rife. *The History of the American Bureau of Shipping: 150th Anniversary*, 7. Houston: ABS, 2013, http://ww2.eagle.org/content/dam/eagle/publications/2012/ABSHistory150.pdf.

Falk, John H., and Lynn D. Dierking. *The Museum Experience*. Washington, D.C.: Whalesback Books, 1992.

Falk, John, and Lynn Dierking. *Learning from Museums: Visitor Experiences and the Making of Meaning*. Lanham, MD: AltaMira, 2000.

Fergus, Robert, ed. *Chicago River and Harbor Convention: An Account of Its Origins and Proceedings*. Chicago: Fergus Printing, 1882.

Florida Bureau of Archaeological Research. "A Proposal to Establish the Shipwreck USS *Narcissus* as a State Underwater Archaeological Preserve." Tallahassee: Florida Bureau of Archaeological Research, 2011.

Friday, Joe D. Jr. "The History, Archaeology, and Current Status of the Wreck of the USS *Huron*." In *Underwater Archaeology Proceedings from the Society for Historical Archaeology Conference*, edited by John D. Broadwater, 51–53. Germantown, MD: Society for Historical Archaeology, 1991.

Funk, Susan S. Interview by the author. Mystic Seaport Museum, Mystic, CT. January 19, 2016.

George, Rose. *Ninety Percent of Everything: Inside Shipping, the Invisible Industry.* New York: Metropolitan Books, 2013.

Georgopoulos, Panagotis, and Tatiana Fragkopoulou. "Underwater Archaeological Parks in Greece: The Cases of Methoni Bay—Sapienza Island and Northern Sporades, from a Culture of Prohibition to a Culture of Engagement." In *ACUA Underwater Archaeology Proceedings 2013*, edited by Colin Breen and Wes Forsythe, 191–96. Germantown, MD: Advisory Council on Underwater Archaeology, 2013.

German, Andrew W. "'Seasoned and Weather-Stained,' How the Charles W. Morgan Lives at Age 150." *Sea History* 60 (Winter 1991–1992): 10–12.

Gibbins, David and Jonathan Adams. "Shipwrecks and Maritime Archaeology." *World Archaeology* 32(3) (2001): 279–91.

González-Tennant, Edward. "Towards an IQ-GIS for Historical Archaeology," 2014. Accessed December 26, 2015, http://www.gonzaleztennant.net/iq-gis-nevis/.

Gordon, Joseph. "The Morgan's Last Stowaway." *The Log of Mystic Seaport* 25(4) (1973): 122–28.

Haldimand, Frederick. "Letter to Dederick Brehm, 23 July 1779." Michigan Pioneer & Historical Society Collections. 2nd ed., vol. 9. Lansing, MI: Wynkoop Hallenbeck Crawford Company, 1908.

Ham, Sam H. *Interpretation: Making a Difference on Purpose.* Golden, CO: Fulcrum, 2013.

Hannahs, Todd. "Underwater Parks vs. Preserves: Data or Access." In *Submerged Cultural Resource Management: Preserving and Interpreting Our Sunken Maritime Heritage*, edited by James D. Spirek and Della A. Scott-Ireton, 14. New York: Kluwer Academic/Plenum Press, 2003.

Hanselmann, Frederick H., and Charles D. Beeker. "Establishing Marine Protected Areas in the Dominican Republic: A Model for Sustainable Preservation." In *ACUA Underwater Archaeology Proceedings 2008*, edited by Susan Langley and Victor Mastone, 52–61. Germantown, MD: Advisory Council on Underwater Archaeology, 2008.

Harlaftis, Gelina. "Maritime History or the History of *Thalassa.*" In *The New Ways of History*, edited by Gelina Harlaftis, Nikos Karapidakis, Kostas Sbonias, and Vaios Vaiopoulus. London: IB Tauris, 2009.

Harrison, Daniel. "Frontier Arms Race: Historical and Archaeological Analysis of an Assemblage of 18th-Century Cannon Recovered from the Detroit River and Lake Erie." *Historical Archaeology* 48(4) (2014): 27–45.

Hein, George. "The Challenge and Significance of Constructivism." Last modified 2002. Accessed February 15, 2016, http://george-hein.com/papers_online/hoe_2001.html. It was originally published in "Proceedings, Hands On! Europe Conference," 2001, London: Discover, 35–42.

"History of Mystic Seaport—1970s." Mystic Seaport Museum, Inc. Accessed February 13, 2016, http://www.mysticseaport.org/about/history/1970s/.

"History of Mystic Seaport—1990s." Mystic Seaport Museum, Inc. Accessed February 15, 2016, http://www.mysticseaport.org/about/history/1990s/.

Hollander, Neil, and Harald Mertes. *The Last Sailors: The Final Days of Working Sail.* New York: St. Martin's, 1984.

Hugill, Stan, ed. *Shanties from the Seven Seas: Shipboard Work Songs and Songs Used as Work-Songs from the Great Days of Sail.* London: Routledge, 1984 (2nd ed.).

Institute of Museum and Library Services (IMLS). "Government Double Official Estimate: There Are 35,000 Active Museums in the U.S." Accessed February 2016, https://www.imls.gov/news-events/news-releases/government-doubles-official-estimate-there-are-35000-active-museums-us.

———. "Distribution of Museums by Discipline." Accessed February 2016, https://www.imls
.gov/assets/1/AssetManager/MUDF_TypeDist_2014q3.pdf.

International Maritime Organization (IMO). *World Maritime Day 2016*, http://www.imo.org/
en/About/Events/WorldMaritimeDay/Pages/WMD-2016.aspx.

James, Alison. "Researching, Protecting and Managing England's Marine Historic Environment."
In *ACUA Underwater Archaeology Proceedings 2013*, edited by Charles Dagneau and Karolyn
Gauvin, 177. Germantown, MD: Advisory Council on Underwater Archaeology, 2013.

Kilgore, W. F. "Letter to Commander US Steamer." *Sagamore*, January 8, 1866. Record Group
45, HG—Groundings, Strandings, Founderings, and Sinkings. Box No. 179. US Steamer
Althea. Washington, D.C.: Office of Naval Records and Library.

Kipling, Rudyard. *Letters of Travel, 1892–1913*. New York: Doubleday, Page, 1920.

Kohl, Cris. *Shipwreck Tales: The St Clair River (to 1900)*. Chatham, ON: Mercury Press, 1987.

Langley, Susan B. M. "Historic Shipwreck Preserves in Maryland." In *Submerged Cultural Resource
Management: Preserving and Interpreting Our Sunken Maritime Heritage*, edited by James D.
Spirek and Della Scott-Ireton, 45–55. New York: Kluwer Academic/Plenum Press, 2003.

La Roche, Daniel. "A Review of Cultural Resource Management Experiences in Presenting Canada's Submerged Heritage," in *Submerged Cultural Resource Management: Preserving and Interpreting Our Sunken Maritime Heritage*, edited by James D. Spirek and Della Scott-Ireton,
19–41. New York: Kluwer Academic/Plenum Press, 2003.

Lawrence, Richard. "From National Tragedy to Cultural Treasure: The USS *Huron* Historic Ship-
wreck Preserve." In *Submerged Cultural Resource Management: Preserving and Interpreting Our
Sunken Maritime Heritage*, edited by James D. Spirek and Della Scott-Ireton, 69. New York:
Kluwer Academic/Plenum Press, 2003.

Lehrer, Emily, and Cynthia E. Milton, eds. *Curating Difficult Knowledge: Violent Pasts in Public
Places*. London: Palgrave Macmillan, 2011.

Lord, Barry. *The Manual of Museum Learning*. Lanham, MD: AltaMira, 2015.

Lynch, Edmund E. "Memorandum, Re: CHARLES W. MORGAN and Lift Dock," September
1968. Mystic Seaport Museum.

Mahan, Alfred Thayer. *The Influence of Sea Power on History, 1660–1783*. London: Little, Brown,
1890.

Manders, Martijn. "In Situ Preservation: 'The Preferred Option.'" *Museum International* 60(4)
(2009): 31–41.

Mansfield, John Brandt, ed. *History of the Great Lakes*. 2 vol. Chicago: J.H. Beers, 1899.

Maritime Administration and the U.S. Marine Transportation System. "A Vision for the 21st
Century." Accessed February 2016, http://www.marad.dot.gov/wp-content/uploads/pdf/
Vision_of_the_21st_Century_10-29.pdf.

McKinnon, Jennifer F., and Toni L. Carrell, eds. *The Underwater Archaeology of a Pacific Battlefield: The Battle of Saipan*. New York: Springer, 2015.

McLean, Kathleen. "Do Museum Exhibitions Have a Future?" In *Reinventing the Museum*, edited
by Gail Anderson, 291–301. Lanham, MD: AltaMira, 2012.

Memet, Jean-Bernard. "Conservation of Underwater Cultural Heritage: Characteristics and New
Technologies." *Museum International* 60(4) (2008): 42–49.

Merritt, Elizabeth. "Setting the Stage," *Building the Future of Education*. Accessed September 2016,
http://www.aam-us.org/docs/default-source/center-for-the-future-of-museums/building
-the-future-of-education-museums-and-the-learning-ecosystem.pdf?sfvrsn=2.

Monteiro, Alexandre. *Underwater Archaeological Trails and Preserves in Portugal* (Lisbon: Instituto
de Arqueologia e Paleociências, Faculdade de Ciências Sociais e Humanas, Universidade Nova
de Lisboa, 2013).

Morris, Melissa N. T. "USS *Narcissus*: The Role of the Tugboat in the American Civil War." M.A. thesis, University of West Florida, 2011.

Moulton, R., and S. Theime. *History of Dredging and Compensation: St. Clair and Detroit Rivers.* Ottawa, ON: International Upper Great Lakes Study, 2009.

Murphy, Larry. "Shipwrecks as Data Base for Human Behavioral Studies." In *Shipwreck Anthropology*, edited by Richard A. Gould, 65–90. Albuquerque: University of New Mexico Press, 1983.

National Marine Manufacturers Association 1998 report. http://oceanservice.noaa.gov/websites/retiredsites/natdia_pdf/14boatus.pdf; 2010 report at http://www.nmma.org/press/article/18028.

"Naval Intelligence: Changes in the Various Squadrons—Movement of the Vessels." *New York Times*, January 22, 1866, p. 2.

"Navy Bulletin." *New York Herald*, February 6, 1866, p. 8.

Nelson, Bruce. *Workers on the Waterfront.* Urbana: University of Illinois Press, 1988.

Nutley, D. M. "Ten Years of Shipwreck Access and Management Practices," in *Maritime Archaeology in Australia: A Reader*, edited by M. Staniforth and M. Hyde, 277–81. Blackwood, Australia: Southern Archaeology, 2001.

Nutley, David. "Submerged Cultural Sites: Opening a Time Capsule." *Museum International* 60(4) (2008): 7–17.

O'Shea, John M., and Guy A. Meadows. "Evidence for Early Hunters Beneath the Great Lakes." *Proceedings of the National Academy of Sciences*, 2009. Accessed December 26, 2015, http://www.pnas.org/content/106/25/10120.full.pdf.

O'Shea, John M., Ashley K. Lemke, Elizabeth P. Sonnenburg, Robert G. Reynolds, and Brian D. Abbott. "A 9,000-Year-Old Caribou Hunting Structure beneath Lake Huron." *Proceedings of the National Academy of Sciences*, 2014. Accessed December 26, 2015, www.pnas.org/cgi/content/short/1404404111.

Oxley, Ian. "Who Owns England's Marine Historic Assets and Why Does It Matter? English Heritage's Work towards Understanding the Opportunities and Threats, and the Development of Solutions and Constructive Engagement with Owners." In *ACUA Underwater Archaeology Proceedings 2014*, edited by Charles Dagneau and Karolyn Gauvin, 229–33. Germantown, MD: Advisory Council on Underwater Archaeology, 2014.

Paine, Lincoln. "Beyond Dead Whales: Literature of the Sea and Maritime History." *International Journal of Maritime History* 221 no. 1 (June 2010): 205–8.

Pearce, Susan M. "Objects as Meaning; or Narrating the Past." In *Interpreting Objects and Collections*, 19–29. London: Routledge, 1994.

Phillips-Birt, Douglas. *An Eye for a Yacht.* London: Faber & Faber, 1955.

Porter, David Dixon. *The Naval History of the Civil War.* New York: Sherman Publishing Company, 1886.

Price, Franklin H. "Florida's Underwater Archaeological Preserves: Public Participation as an Approach to Submerged Heritage Management." *Public Archaeology* 12(4) (2013): 221–41.

———. "Florida's Underwater Archaeological Preserves 2013 Visitation and Conditions Assessment." Tallahassee: Florida Bureau of Archaeological Research, 2014.

———. "Florida's Underwater Archaeological Preserves 2014 Visitation and Conditions Assessment." Tallahassee: Florida Bureau of Archaeological Research, 2015.

Price, Franklin H., and Nathan Richards. "Conflict and Commerce: Maritime Archaeological Site Distribution as Cultural Change on the Roanoke River, North Carolina." *Historical Archaeology* 43, no. 4 (2009): 75–96.

Purdy, Steven M. "Charles W. Morgan Interpretation Handbook." Unpublished manuscript, Mystic Seaport Museum, Mystic, CT, 2014.

Rose, Julia. *Interpreting Difficult History at Museums and Historic Sites*. Lanham, MD: Rowman & Littlefield, 2016.

Schlereth, Thomas J., ed. *Material Culture Studies in America*. Lanham, MD: AltaMira, 1999.

Scott-Ireton, Della. "Florida's Underwater Archaeological Preserves." *Submerged Cultural Resource Management: Preserving and Interpreting Our Sunken Maritime Heritage*, edited by James D. Spirek and Della Scott-Ireton, 101. New York: Kluwer Academic/Plenum Press, 2003.

———. "Preserves, Parks, and Trails: Strategy and Response in Submerged Cultural Resource Management." PhD diss., Florida State University, 2005.

———. "The Value of Public Education and Interpretation in Submerged Cultural Resource Management." In *Out of the Blue: Public Interpretation of Maritime Cultural Resources*, edited by James H. Jameson Jr. and Della A. Scott-Ireton, 19–32. New York: Springer, 2007.

"Shipwrecks: Loss of the United States Steamer *Narcissus*, with All on Board." *New York Herald*, February 4, 1866, 1.

Silverstone, Paul H. *Warships of the Civil War Navies*. Annapolis, MD: Naval Institute Press, 1989.

Simon, Nina. *The Participatory Museum*. Santa Cruz, CA: Museum 2.0, 2010.

Smith, Joshua M. "Far Beyond Jack Tar: Maritime Historians and the Problem of Audience." *Coriolis* 2(2) (2011): 1. Accessed February 2016, http://ijms.nmdl.org/article/view/9836.

Smith, Roger C. "Memorandum re: *San Pedro* Wreck Site and Park Update." November 7, 1988. Tallahassee, FL: Bureau of Archaeological Research, 1988.

———. "Florida's Underwater Archaeological Preserves." In *Underwater Archaeology Proceedings from the Society for Historical Archaeology Conference 1991*, edited by John D. Broadwater, 43–46. Germantown, MD: Society for Historical Archaeology, 1991.

———. "Foreword." In *Submerged Cultural Resource Management: Preserving and Interpreting Our Sunken Maritime Heritage*, edited by James D. Spirek and Della A. Scott-Ireton, vii–viii. New York: Kluwer Academic/Plenum Press, 2003.

Smith, Robert H. *Maritime Museums of North America and Canada*. New York: Finley-Greene Publications, 1998.

———. *Maritime Museums of North America and Canada*. New York: Finley-Greene Publications, 2007. Accessed February 2016, http://www.maritimemuseums.net/.

Smith, Sheli O. "Frolic *Archaeological Survey*." Columbus, OH: PAST Foundation, 2005.

St. Lucie County Board of Commissioners, Letter to Senator Robert Williams, 24 April 1968, Florida Master Site File, Tallahassee.

Stackpole, Edouard A. *The Charles W. Morgan: The Last Wooden Whaleship*. New York: Meredith Press, 1967.

Steers, MacDonald, ed. *Mystic Seaport Guide*. Mystic, CT: Marine Historical Association, 1952.

Stefanile, Michele. "Research, Protection, and Musealization in an Underwater Archaeological Park: The Case of Baia (Naples, Italy)." In *Actas de las IV Jornadas de Jovens em Investigação Arqueológica*, 57–63. Faro: Promontoria Monográfica, 2012.

Suchy, Sherene. *Leading with Passion: Change Management in the 21st Century Museum*. Walnut Creek, CA: AltaMira, 2004.

Tikkanen, Sallamaria. "Case Studies of Existing Underwater Trails." In *Nordic Blue Parks: Nordic Perspectives on Underwater Natural and Cultural Heritage*, edited by K. O'Brien, S. Tikkannen, C. Lindblad, P. Flyg, A. Olsson, O. Uldum, I. Aarestad, and D. Naevdal, 19–32. Copenhagen: Nordic Council of Ministers, 2011.

Tilden, Freeman. *Interpreting Our Heritage*. 4th ed. Chapel Hill: University of North Carolina Press, 2007.

Tunell, George. "Transportation of the Great Lakes of North America." *Journal of Political Economy* 4(3) (1896): 332–51.

Tusa, Sebastiano. "Research, Protection and Evaluation of Sicilian and Mediterranean Cultural Heritage." *Conservation Science in Cultural Heritage* 2009(9): 79–112.

United Nations. "Contribution of the International Maritime Organization (IMO) to the Secretary-General's Report on Oceans and the Law of the Sea, 2008," http://www.un.org/depts/los/consultative_process/mar_sec_submissions/imo.pdf.

United Nations Educational, Scientific and Cultural Organization (UNESCO). Information Kit: UNESCO Convention on the Protection of the Underwater Cultural Heritage. Paris: UNESCO, 2001. Accessed December 26, 2015, http://unesdoc.unesco.org/images/0014/001430/143085e.pdf.

"The United States Steamer *Narcissus*: Further Details from Ensign Lannan." *New York Times*, February 4, 1866, p. 8.

US Central Intelligence Agency. *World Factbook*. Washington, D.C.: Central Intelligence Agency, 2010, https://www.cia.gov/library/publications/the-world-factbook/rankorder/2108rank.html#us.

US Navy. *Status of the Navy*. Washington, D.C.: US Navy, 2015, http://www.navy.mil/navydata/nav_legacy.asp?id=146.

Vickers, Daniel. "Beyond Jack Tar." *William and Mary Quarterly* (3rd Series) 50(2) (April 1993): 418–24.

Weekley, Ernest. *An Etymological Dictionary of Modern English*. New York: Dover Publications, 1967.

Weil, Stephen E. "From Being about Something to Being for Somebody: The Ongoing Transformation of the American Museum." Harvard University. http://isites.harvard.edu/fs/docs/icb.topic862568.files/Supplementary%20Readings/Weil%201999.pdf. Originally, Weil, Stephen E. "From Being about Something to Being for Somebody: The Ongoing Transformation of the American Museum." *Daedalus* 128, no. 3 (1999): 229–59.

Wells, Pat. "Crisis and Miscellaneous Incident Report No. A38386: *San Pedro* Underwater Archaeological Preserve." Florida Department of Natural Resources, 1995.

Wilde-Ramsing, Mark, and Lauren Hermley. "Diver Awareness Program: QAR Dive Down." In *Out of the Blue: Public Interpretation of Maritime Cultural Resources*, edited by John H. Jameson and Della Scott-Ireton, 127–44. New York: Springer, 2007.

Wilkening, Susie. *Annual Demographic Update*. Glenmont, NY: REACH Advisors, 2014.

Why the "Morgan" Came to Mystic. Mystic, CT: Marine Historical Association, 1942.

Zarzynski, Joseph W. "Lake George, New York: Making Shipwrecks Speak." In *Out of the Blue: Public Interpretation of Maritime Cultural Resources*, edited by John H. Jameson and Della Scott-Ireton, 19–32. New York: Springer, 2007.

Zarzynski, Joseph W., David J. Decker, Peter J. Pepe, and Steven C. Resler. "Painting the Water Blue: The New York State Underwater Blueway Trail." In *ACUA Underwater Archaeology Proceedings 2007*, edited by Victor Mastone, 151–56. Germantown, MD: Advisory Council on Underwater Archaeology, 2007.

INDEX

Abandoned Shipwreck Act 1988, 72
Abbe Museum, 144
advertising, 147
Alvin Clark, 6
Amistad, 37
American Bureau of Shipping, 16, 18
American Canoe Association, 114
American Civil War, 14–16, 65, 71
American Revolutionary War, 89
Andrea Doria, 18
Antique and Classic Boat Society, 112
Antique Boat Museum, 112, 119–23
Apalachicola Maritime Museum, 144
art, 147
Avalon, 47

Bayview Yacht Club, 58; Port Huron to Macki-
    nac Race, 67
Belle of Louisville, 6, 9, 45–56
Bluenose, 4

Canadian Canoe Museum, *122*, 123, 144
Canadian Shipowners Association, 143
canoeing, 113–15, *122*, 123
Carleton, Sir Guy, 90
Carl D. Bradley, 105
Célèbre, 74
Charles W. Morgan, 9, 31–44
City of Hawkinsville, 74
Clearwater, 6
Columbia River Maritime Museum, 144
commemoration, 142–43

Copenhagen, 75, *78*
Coronation, 73
Council of American Maritime Museums
    (CAMM), 6
Chris-Craft, 18, 58, 112
Cranbrook Institute of Science, 63, 88
cruise ships, 19, 146

Daniel J. Morrell, 105
David Boyd, 108
Detroit & Cleveland Navigation Company, 58
Detroit Historical Museum, 61
Detroit Historical Society, 10, 57–61
Detroit Police Department Underwater Recov-
    ery Team, 88
Detroit River, *86*
Detroit River cannon, *87*
difficult topics, 135–39
diving, 71–81, 146
Dossin Great Lakes Museum, 4, 10, 57–69, 91,
    142–43
Duckenfield, 74

Eastland, 17
Edmund Fitzgerald, 102, *104*, 142, 143
Emergency Fleet Corporation, 16
Empress of Ireland, 17
Erie, *93*
exhibition design: audience evaluation, 11n2,
    39, 50, 55, 60–62, 69, 80; challenges, 35–36,
    51–54, 58, 80–81; complimentary program-
    ming, 37, 51, 55–56, 130–134; interactive,

40, 67; interpretation, 8, 23, 27–28, 39–41, 50–69, 77–79, 91–92, 94–97, 119–23, 144; music, 35–36, 40, 122–23, 125–34; technology, 41–42, 78–79, 96, 129

Fairport Harbor Marine Museum, 4
Fisherman's Wharf, 4
Florida Aquarium, 76
Florida Historical Resources Act 1967, 72
Florida Public Archaeology Network, 76
Florida Underwater Archaeological Preserves, 10, 73, 75–81
Fort Lernoult, 89
Fort Malden, 90
Fort Pontchartrain, 88–89
Fort William Historical Park, 144
France, 18

Gardner, John, 112
Georges Valentine, 75, *76*
Gorsage, J. Herod, 47
Great Lakes Maritime Institute, 61
Great Lakes Shipwreck Historical Society, 10, 100
Great Lakes Shipwreck Museum, *91*, 99–109, *103*
Gryphon, 108

Hale, Dennis, 105, *106*
Half Moon, 74
Hazardous, 73
Hillman Brothers, 33
Historic Memorials Committee, 61
Historical Society of the Great Lakes, 62
HMS *Colossus*, 73
Huron, 74

Idlewild, 45–47
immigration, 139
Independence Seaport, 4
International Maritime Organization (IMO), 20n9
International Shipmasters' Association, 61, 143

J.T. Wing, 58
J.W. Westcott II, 58

James Rees and Sons, 45
Jones Act, 17
Jones, Senator Wesley, 16–17

Kentucky Derby Festival Great Steamboat Race 1963, 49
Kipling, Rudyard, 85
Kronprinz Gustav, 74

La Follette Seaman's Act, 17
Lake Carriers' Association, 94, 143
Lake Champlain Maritime Museum, 144
Leighton, Ryan, 42
Life-Saving Station #10, 51
Lofthus, 75
Luckenbach, J. Lewis, 18
Lyman, 112
Lusitania, 17

MacGregor, John, 113, 114
Massachusetts Maritime Academy, 40
Marine Historical Association. *See* Mystic Seaport
Marine Historical Society of Detroit, 61
Mariners' Museum, 4
Merchant Marine Act. *See* Jones Act
Michigan Audubon Society, 109
Michigan Humanities Council, 105
Museums in the Sea, 78–79
Museum of the Great Lakes. *See* Dossin Great Lakes Museum
Mystic Seaport, 6, 9, 31–44, 112

National Endowment for the Humanities (NEH), 39, 41
National Oceanic and Atmospheric Administration (NOAA), 39
Narragansett Boat Club, 114
Native Americans, 11, 65, 143–44
New Bedford Whaling Museum, 39
New York Canoe Club, 114

Pier Wisconsin, 4
piracy, 137
Pride of Baltimore, 4
Protected Wrecks Act (Great Britain), 74

Queen Anne's Revenge, 74

recreational boating, 66–68, 111–23, 147
Regina, 75
Rob Roy, 113
Rose Island Company, 46
Royal Canoe Club, 114

Safety of Life at Sea (SOLAS), 18
San Pedro, 74
Savannah, 18
scuba. *See* diving
SeaRay, 58
ships: commerce, 14–20, 21; design, 13–16,
    23–25, 115–19; propulsion, 25–26, *118*;
    terminology, 22–23; warfare, 12–18
shipwreck(s): as interpretive tool, 77–78,
    92–97, 137; legislation,73, 77, 81n4
slavery, 138–139
Sopritendenza del Mare, 74
South Street Seaport, 4
Southeastern Archaeological Services, 77
Spirit of Jefferson, 51
St. Clair Flats, *86*, 92–97
St. Clair River, *86*
St. Louis and Calhoun Packet Company, 47
St. Lucie County Historical Commission, 75
Sunken Military Craft Act 2005, 77
surfing, 144

Tarpon, 74
technology. *See* exhibition design
Titanic, 17
Tripp, Captain William Henry, 31–32

U-1105, 74
Urca de Lima, 74

Underground Railroad, 11, 61, 65, 144–46
United Nations, 18
United States, 18
US Army Corps of Engineers, 93
US Central Intelligence Agency, 19
US Coast Guard, 52–53, 77, 100, 142, 143
US Department of Commerce, 94
US Department of the Interior, 49
US Fish and Wildlife Service, 109
US Life-Saving Service, 100, *102*
US Lighthouse Service, 100
US Maritime Commission, 17
US Merchant Marine, 19
US Merchant Marine Academy, 18
US National Parks Service, 73
US Navy, 14–18, 142
US Navy History and Heritage Command, 77
US Treasury Department, 19
USS *Althea*, 71
USS *Arizona*, 73
USS *Constitution*, 39
USS *Massachusetts*, 74
USS *Narcissus*, 71–72, 75

Vamar, 74

Walton, Ivan, 126
War of 1812, 14, 65,
West Memphis Packet Company, 45
whaling, 31–44, 138
Whitefish Point. *See* Great Lakes Shipwreck
    Museum
Wilson, Loudon, 126
William Clay Ford, 64
Wooden Canoe Heritage Association, 123
World War I, 16
World War II, 17–18, 47

ABOUT THE EDITOR AND CONTRIBUTORS

Kadie Engstrom has worked with the historic river steamboat *Belle of Louisville* for nearly half a century. As Education Coordinator she has developed and facilitated countless educational experiences on river, steamboat, or local history for children and adults, including community presentations and exhibits, classroom and on-board programs for students, professional development workshops for teachers, and on-board narrations for special-interest groups and public cruises. Kadie currently serves as chair of the Kentuckiana Heritage Consortium, and is author of *Pathway through the Past: A Timeline of the Development of History in the Louisville Metropolitan Area.*

Daniel Harrison is a reference librarian at Henry Ford College in Dearborn, Michigan. A doctoral candidate in anthropology at Wayne State University, his earlier research led to the listing of a submerged supply road from the War of 1812—Hull's Trace—on the National Register of Historic Places, and its inclusion in 2014 as a unit of the River Raisin National Battlefield Park. His presentations and writing centers on the maritime archaeology of the Great Lakes, and he is familiar with bottomland resources in the North American Midwest.

Erik Ingmundson is the Supervisor of Interpretation at Mystic Seaport: The Museum of America and the Sea. He was instrumental in the historic tour of the century-old American whaleship *Charles W. Morgan* from its birth in Mystic Harbor to other fabled whaling ports. Born in Maine, he studied history at Wheaton College, and worked as an interpreter at Nantucket's Whaling Museum before completing a degree in Public History at the University of Massachusetts. Erik is a 2015 graduate of the American Association of State and Local History's Developing History Leaders @ SHA program.

Bruce Lynn is the executive director of the Great Lakes Shipwreck Museum on Whitefish Point along the eastern coast of Lake Superior. With degrees from Ohio State University, and Eastern Michigan University in historic preservation and interpretation, Bruce has experience at the Mackinac Island Historic Parks and the Alfred P. Sloan Museum in

Flint, Michigan. He recently cowrote *The Legend Lives On*, about the SS *Edmund Fitzgerald*, with Christopher Winters for the Great Lakes Shipwreck Historical Society.

Lee Murdock and **Joann Murdock** have performed and promoted maritime music for nearly four decades. Together they have produced over twenty albums of maritime music—traditional and original—celebrating the tales and fortunes of people who relied on ships for a livelihood. Lee does the writing, picking, and singing. Joann handles marketing, licensing and scheduling for Lee and a number of other artists. They published *Lake Rhymes: Folk Songs of the Great Lakes Region* in 2004, and were part of the *Windjammer: Songs of the Great Lakes Sailors* project in 2002.

Making folk music for the modern era, Lee Murdock's work is a documentary and also an anthem to the people who live, work, learn, and play along the freshwater highways of North America. Traveling thousands of miles a year in order to bring people the music of the Great Lakes maritime, Lee won the 2016 Joyce Hayward Award for Historic Interpretation from the Association for Great Lakes Maritime History.

Franklin H. Price is the senior archaeologist with the Florida Department of State's Bureau of Archaeological Research. A native of Maine, he has a BA from Earlham College in Richmond, Indiana, and an MA in maritime studies from East Carolina University. His experience in underwater archaeology includes both maritime and inundated prehistoric projects. Franklin is widely published and coordinates public outreach, and dive operations, and manages Florida's Underwater Archaeological Preserve program and the *Museum of the Sea* project.

Joel Stone, editor of this volume, is senior curator with the Detroit Historical Society, which manages the Detroit Historical Museum, the Dossin Great Lakes Museum, and a significant collection of both archival and physical maritime artifacts. Besides attending to the rich trove of Detroit history, he specializes in the matters of the North American maritime. Joel recently had *Palace Steamers of the Great Lakes: A History of Passenger Steamships on the Inland Seas* published by the University of Michigan Press.

John Summers has spent decades devoted to promoting the recreational aspects of maritime history. After graduating from the University of Toronto with an advanced degree in museum studies, he served as Curator of the Marine Museum of Upper Canada and The Pier: Toronto's Waterfront Museum. During a decade in the United States, he was Curator for the International Yacht Restoration School, then Chief Curator of the Antique Boat Museum in Clayton, New York. Following a return to Canada in 2008, he spent five years as General Manager of the Canadian Canoe Museum in Peterborough, Ontario, and is now Manager of Heritage Services and Curator for the Regional Municipality of Halton, Ontario. Widely published, and a regular contributor to *Wooden Boat* magazine, he also builds and restores wooden boats and blogs about his interests at authenticboats.com.